THE SONG
OF THE
BODY

Dance for Lifelong Wellbeing

PATRON: HER MAJESTY QUEEN ELIZABETH II

EDITED BY DR ANNE HOGAN
FOREWORD BY DARCEY BUSSELL

2

Contents

Acknowledgements

The Song of the Body: Dance for Lifelong Wellbeing is a collective endeavour, and I am deeply grateful to the many champions of dance as a potent means of enhancing wellbeing who contributed to its production. I'd like to thank, first of all, the contributors to the panel discussions, profiles, interviews and articles for so generously giving their time and sharing their expertise and insights. I'd also like to acknowledge the members of the Faculty of Education at the Royal Academy of Dance (RAD) and the participants in our pilot project for older learners, which served as the catalyst for a subsequent conference on dance for lifelong wellbeing, and this publication. Dr Carol Martin and Dr Victoria Watts provided invaluable input to the initial preparation of this book. I'm also indebted to my colleagues across the RAD for so enthusiastically supporting the project, and wish to give particular thanks to Aiden Truss, a contributor and copy writer for the RAD, and Sarah Bailey for their assistance with the editing process. My thanks also to Melanie Murphy and Sue Bacchus for their invaluable support of the production and promotion of this work.

Dr Anne Hogan
Director of Education, Royal Academy of Dance

Foreword

**BY DARCEY BUSSELL, PRESIDENT
OF THE ROYAL ACADEMY OF DANCE**

This important book grew out of the Dance for Lifelong Wellbeing Conference in 2013 that showcased initiatives which went well beyond the usual work of the RAD. It highlighted dance as a means of enhancing lives through improving both social and physical wellbeing.

I am the most passionate advocate of the power of dance as a force for inspiring people, regardless of age and situation, to change their lives and communities for the better.

The stories and case studies in this book show the wide variety of ways in which people engage with dance to enrich their lives whether as a career, for fitness or just as a way to get out and make new friends. It also suggests ways in which we might harness its holistic benefits to serve the physical, social and perhaps even spiritual good.

Above all, this book shows that dance is not just for the theatre or the studio; it needs to permeate every aspect of society. Dance provides an outlet and a form of expression that can bring fulfilment and joy to everyone who takes part.

Introduction

DR ANNE HOGAN, DIRECTOR OF EDUCATION AT THE ROYAL ACADEMY OF DANCE

From the philosophical axioms of the ancient schools of wisdom to the recent propositions of positive psychology, the meaning of wellbeing has been ceaselessly, and as yet inconclusively, debated. Aristotle, for one, eschewed its equation with mere happiness, suggesting instead that our highest good ('eudaimonia') lies in leading a virtuous life and doing what is right. Speculation about precisely what that might consist of, or whether virtue is indeed an efficacious conduit to wellbeing, has further fuelled incalculable hypotheses and lifestyle prescriptions.

Martin Seligman, one of positive psychology's most influential proponents, has moved from an earlier emphasis on 'authentic happiness' to a more holistic understanding of wellbeing as getting the most out of life, or 'flourishing,' the essential elements of which are neatly encapsulated within the acronym PERMA: Positive emotion, Engagement, Relationships, Meaning and Achievement. Seligman's concept is intriguingly comprehensive, aligning as it does the subjective and the relational, but no doubt it will not be the final word on the significance of wellbeing. The slipperiness of the term has proved ironically commensurate with its predominance as a human pursuit.

The Song of the Body hardly presumes to delimit the parameters of wellbeing, but rather to celebrate dance as a powerful means of enhancing it in all its intricate and inter-fused varieties: physical, emotional, spiritual, and intellectual. The book aims to give a collective, if not necessarily uniform, voice to dance as a tool by which to accelerate one's capacity for vitality and abundance at all stages of the life cycle. The joy of movement that many of the contributors touch upon surpasses a superficial, feel-good buzz: dance, they believe, can allow our channels of perception to hum intensely, passionately in tandem. Dance, this book suggests, can change your life, at any phase, in amazing – and sometimes unanticipated – ways.

The Song of the Body can trace its origins to a research and outreach project for older learners, for which the Faculty of Education at the Royal Academy of Dance (RAD) received funding in the summer of 2012. This was from the Community Learning Innovation Fund (financed by the Skills Funding Agency and managed by the National Institute for Adult

Photo credit Peter Bartlett.

dance classes to older learners in a variety of community settings. This in turn accommodated a small scale, qualitative research initiative aimed towards assessing the impact of dance on the health and wellbeing of older adults.

As the Director of Education at the RAD, I had the pleasure of observing firsthand the enthusiasm with which the teachers, and the RAD colleagues who offered them peer mentoring and support, embraced the opportunity to engage with older learners (the eldest of whom was a sprightly 102 years of age). Indeed, their initial enthusiasm morphed into something nearing awe as they witnessed the joy, creativity and social cohesion the dance sessions fostered among the older participants. The playful ambience of the classes seemed particularly poignant in light of increasing evidence suggesting that loneliness and isolation, exacerbated by cuts to local services such as day centres and lunch clubs, may be the greatest detriment to the health of older adults ("Loneliness on the rise among the elderly"). Isolation can not only lead to poor eating habits and less motivation to be physically active, it can even damage the immune system, leading to illnesses such as chronic inflammation.

To be sure, the sense of collaborative fun in learning new moves emerged for some of the participants by degrees – step by step, as it were. The video documentation, teachers' notes and the learner's reports, however, suggested improved physical wellbeing, although further research will be necessary to more precisely ascertain corporeal gain. What was more readily evident, however, as the participants

Continuing Education). The project was led by Dr Victoria Watts, whose reflections on the project in light of widespread assumptions about ageing as deterioration are included in this book. Victoria was compelled to initiate the project when she came across data attesting to the shift, as monumental as it is swift, in national and international demographics towards an ageing population (*Dance for Lifelong Wellbeing: Project Report*).

Colleagues in the Faculty of Education were keen to join her in exploring how the RAD's expertise in dance training and education could contribute to ensuring that the exponentially escalating sector of older adults can experience ageing as an active, enjoyable and, indeed, empowering process. As Vicki's article details, the ensuing pilot project comprised of training for six experienced dance teachers to deliver laughed together, delighting in the use of props and the catchy tunes to which they swayed, was the power of dance to enhance social and emotional wellbeing. Dancing simply made the older learners feel great – and the teachers who danced with them had a wonderful time, too!

As the project approached the conclusion of its pilot phase, my RAD colleagues and I were inspired by it to explore the broader potential of dance to enhance the quality of life in every phase of its continuum. To this end, we held a three-day conference in April 2013 on 'Dance for Lifelong Wellbeing'. This was organised around three key constituencies: young people, adults (including older adults) and the professional dance community. The resulting panel discussions and presentations highlighted RAD expertise and initiatives with regard to each, such as RADiate, which offers subsidised dance classes to children on the autistic spectrum, Step into Dance, which brings dance provision to 200 schools throughout London and Essex, and the Faculty of Education's portfolio of programmes for professional dancers making the (sometimes emotionally fraught) career transition from performing into teaching. It also brought together high-profile researchers and practitioners from the arts and health science sectors, including representation from partner institutions, government agencies, dance companies and health organisations. The conference aimed to disseminate information and to stimulate debate about the various ways that dance contributes to

the health and wellbeing of people of all ages. It also underscored the need for more dance practitioners to actively engage in national and international investigations of what the concept of wellbeing signifies for an increasingly technological, economically challenged and ageing population. How does, or might, dance matter?

Given the breadth of the topic, the conference but grazed the surface of the conjunction between dance and wellbeing. The opportunity, nonetheless, for stakeholders from a range of disciplines and vantage points to share insights and queries resulted not only in stimulating discussions and but also the forging of new professional networks and collaborative exchange. We uploaded some of the conference presentations to the RAD website (the hilarious, heartening keynote address by the unfailingly spry Gillian Lynne is not to be missed). But we continued to have so many requests to make the panel discussions and other conference content more widely available that we decided to compile a publication drawing upon and augmenting the conference proceedings.

Like the conference that engendered it, *The Song of the Body* considers dance and lifelong wellbeing from the perspectives of the young through to older adults, and also unpacks some of the particular issues related to wellbeing for professional dancers, both young and not so young. While the technical acumen of professional dancers arguably allows them to experience, at least in some ways, a highly refined appreciation of the benefits of dance, they are also particularly prone to the injurious sting of the very art form that sustains them. This book's title, after all, echoes Martha Graham's observation that dance "is a song of the body. Both in joy and pain", and its content as a whole does not endeavour to present a rose-coloured view of dance in relation to health and wellbeing.

Accordingly, the commentary from professional as well as amateur dance practitioners confronts the time and effort that dance proficiency requires, the powerful, sometimes disturbing emotions it can bring forth, and the threat of injury it can pose. Some of the contributors advocate for further advances in safe practice and injury prevention across the dance sector. Others offer practical suggestions for enhancing social integration in the dance studio, and fostering basic understanding of anatomy for dancers. Yet while acknowledging the need for further education and policy change to more broadly instil healthier, safer dance practice, the contributors maintain an overall and unabashed faith in dance as a positive force for lifelong wellbeing.

We begin with four panel discussions, as a means of contextualising the broad scope of issues encompassed within the ensuing interviews, articles, profiles and case studies. *The Song of the Body* is not a compilation of research findings and statistical data about dance and wellbeing, nor is it intended for an exclusively academic audience, though it does refer to ongoing scholarly inquiry. Rather, it could be approached as a potpourri of anecdotes and outlooks; of stories, perhaps,

or as a congregation of contradistinctive reminiscences and opinions, expressed by practitioners engaging with dance from uniquely attuned angles and aspirations. These include dance teachers in the private, community and public sectors, company and vocational school directors, dance project administrators, university lecturers and researchers, and professional and amateur dancers of everything from ballet to hip hop to contemporary and South Asian dance genres. Their common denominator is a passion for dance and a belief that it can make us happier, healthier, more resilient, self aware, socially integrated and maybe even smarter. Dance, the diverse voices that are amassed here suggest, makes us feel more alive.

The commentary and images that comprise *The Song of the Body* need not necessarily be engaged with in a linear fashion – feel free to skip about the book and tease out alternative nuances by juxtaposing its content otherwise. I hope that you may be inspired by the book's array of experiences and viewpoints, and that they help provoke further discourse and research into dance and lifelong wellbeing.

But most of all, I hope you never stop dancing!

References

Watts, Victoria, ed. *Dance for Lifelong Wellbeing: Project Report 2013*. London: Royal Academy of Dance, 2013. Print.

*The project report can be downloaded for free at www.radeducation.org.uk/danceforlifelongwellbeing

"Loneliness on the rise among the elderly". BBC. Web. 3 May 2014. www.bbc.co.uk/news/uk-politics-27247418

PART ONE

DANCING THROUGH LIFE AND LIVING THROUGH DANCE

PANEL DISCUSSIONS FROM
THE RAD DANCE FOR LIFELONG
WELLBEING CONFERENCE

Who Cares? The Health and Wellbeing of Professional Dancers

EDITED BY DR ANNE HOGAN, DIRECTOR OF EDUCATION AT THE ROYAL ACADEMY OF DANCE, PANEL CHAIR

13

Who Cares? The Health and Wellbeing of Professional Dancers

PANELISTS:

Erin Sanchez: *Dance UK Healthier Dancer Programme and administrator of the Rudolf Nureyev Foundation medical website*

Professor Matthew Wyon: *Professor of Dance Science, University of Wolverhampton*

Mark Rasmussen: *Group Marketing Manager, Harlequin Floors*

Kim Amundsen: *Dancer (formerly with Random Dance Company, Bavarian State Ballet and Matthew Bourne's Adventures in Motion Pictures) and Teacher*

Carol Anne Millar: *Dancer (former Principal Dancer, Birmingham Royal Ballet) and Teacher*

…

ANNE: Our panelists bring with them a considerable range of expertise and vantage points from which to discuss health and wellbeing issues for the professional dance sector. Erin, could you begin by telling us a bit about the Dance UK Healthier Dancer Programme – how did it come about, and what does it do?

…

ERIN: Sure. Dance UK is the national membership support organisation for the professional dance sector, set up in 1982 by and for dancers. The Healthier Dancer Programme sits within that and advocates for and supports dancers' health. The HDP, as we call it, held the first conference on dancers' health in 1990. This led to the first national inquiry into dancers' health and injury, which looked at how injury could be prevented and dancers' performing careers could be maximised. The research findings, published in 1996, indicated that roughly 80% of professional dancers are injured each year, and between 50 and 70% of those dancers were paying for their own injury care regardless of their employment status at the time.

…

ANNE: Those are pretty disturbing findings!

…

ERIN: Absolutely, although the legacy of this research was that some of the largest dance companies employed multi-disciplinary teams to look after their dancers' health and fitness. And while small companies are always going to be limited by their financial capabilities, the research helped to argue for the importance of medical insurance, health care and dance science support, and fitness programmes for dancers. Dance UK at that time also started to offer 'road shows', where we brought workshops to companies and schools focusing on dancers' health issues such as fitness, wellbeing, psychology and nutrition. Then in 2005, HDP undertook a second inquiry, looking at much the same questions as the first. This time, the findings indicated that while injury was still a major concern, there were fewer eating problems among dancers, who were also smoking less and were less inclined to ignore injury or put off treatment. In addition, environmental factors such as inadequate floors and dance spaces have reduced thanks to Dance UK's advocacy work across the sector, and invaluable support from proactive corporations, such as Harlequin Floors.

After the second survey findings were published, Helen Laws (manager of the HDP since 2000), started to push for better healthcare for all injured dancers. And in April last year, after raising £120,000, Dance UK launched the National Institute for Dance Medicine and Science, or NIDMS. Our partners were Trinity Laban, the University of Birmingham, Birmingham Royal Ballet, the University of Wolverhampton, and the Royal National Orthopaedic Hospital, with support from the Jerwood Charitable foundation and Harlequin Floors. NIDMS aims to provide access for all dancers to high-quality, evidence-based, dance-specific health science and dance science services, including a dancer's health and injury clinic in the Royal National Orthopaedic Hospital, which is free to all dancers through a referral from their GP.

In 2011, my colleague Niamh Morrin and I took over the management of the HDP and, thanks to that expansion of staff, were able to offer more workshops to more companies and schools and we are busier than ever. So I feel like we've had quite a good history of working with our partners to promote dancers' health.
…

ANNE: Yes, it's very encouraging. Obviously there's a lot yet to be done, but it seems like a tremendous amount of progress has been made by the HDP and its partners. Erin, you spoke a bit about dance injury and prevention, and I'm interested in Matthew's thoughts about this. What impact, in your experience, has the field of dance science had on the day to day working lives of professional dancers?
…

MATTHEW: I'd say varied, fluctuating. One of the biggest problems is that from a historical point of view, science and the arts are quite bipolar, in some ways. Dance was historically taught in schools within physical education departments, and I suppose that when dance science appeared, some dancers and teachers got worried they were being dragged back into the sciences, or PE, again. Sport science has been going since 1954 and it's promoted some quite outstanding performances, as we saw here in London in the last summer Olympics. So there's a very, very close relationship between science and sports performance. When dance science started rearing its head around 1984 and saying,

"Oh, these dancers seem to be working quite hard and what they do looks quite athletic," some dancers didn't like that word. A lot of the dance world still views us quite suspiciously, thinking that we're trying to change dance or, limit creativity. In fact, we're there to try to support dancers and hopefully reduce injuries.

It's been an interesting process. I've seen with great excitement positive measures taken by companies, then there's been a change in artistic director and things go back to the previous environment. And then somebody else comes in and it changes again. But some of the big ballet companies, such as Birmingham Royal Ballet, have had the foresight to utilise the skills and insights from dance science. They looked at the different floors that they were dancing on, for instance, and realised, as we know from sport, that when you change the floor too much, you're going to get more injuries. It's the same with distance runners getting injured when they go from cross-country to running on tracks. So Birmingham Royal Ballet bought a touring floor which had the same resistance as the floors they rehearsed on, and that helped reduce injuries.

...

ANNE: I'd like to hear our dancers' perspectives on these sorts of shifts. Kim and Carol Anne, what changes, if any, have you seen with regard to training? Is there increasing emphasis on promoting injury prevention and overall fitness?

...

KIM: The college I started with in Norway had very strong links to the science department, so from a very early age we got an understanding of how sports training could show you how to more efficiently use your body. Ski jumping technique, for example, could help you do *tour en l'air*. When I moved to Germany, the training was much more rigid and less focused on wellbeing. It was more about forcing turnout to fit a framework, and I ended up feeling weak as a result.

Then I moved to Paris to join a company where they were really into floor barre technique. We did at least a three-quarter of an hour session before our warm-up class, every day, and my body changed dramatically; the sensation of core strength and the use of breath made me feel incredibly free as a performer. Then I joined the English National Ballet, and was hit in the face again with the rigid approach at that time to classicism: of trying to force your body into something that it might not be, and which may not be needed. For a body to look turned out to an audience doesn't mean that you have to force your heels in 5th position towards the edge of the stage. It means that your body needs to be shaped correctly to create an illusion.

Fortunately, I haven't had a lot of injuries in my career, and when I've been a freelance dancer with contemporary companies, I have been in general very well looked after. I've been sent to special orthopaedic clinics where they actually have an interest in the dance. It's not always like that, however. Dancers often rely on word of mouth referrals, trying so many things and spending so much money and often still not getting the right treatment needed at the time. That's why I'm so thrilled about the clinic Erin mentioned, as dancers can now be helped by specialists with an interest in dance. Too often, a dancer will see specialists who'll say, "that's fine now", but what might be fine for running or for walking is not fine for the sort of mobility required in dance. A specialist might sign you off as clear when actually you're not, and working on a half-injury can turn it into a major one.

...

ANNE: That supports Matthew's point about the need for mutual understanding between the science and dance sectors. Kim, you've worked in so many contexts – some of which were quite supportive for dancers and others far less so. Carol Anne, how does that compare with your experience?

...

CAROL ANNE: Well, I'm extremely fortunate because my training was done through the Royal Ballet School, and in my seven years there I was never forced to extremes and never suffered an injury. The training approaches from that time might seem now a bit old-school, but I always felt that we were supported. I joined the Birmingham Royal Ballet in 1997, and I remember our little physio room was basically like a little box. There were two physio beds, a masseur, two physiotherapists, a Pilates space in one of the old studios, and that was it really.

Then the Jerwood Centre was established, and the company was so fortunate to have such a beautiful place devoted to injury prevention and wellbeing. There are three physiotherapists, two masseurs, a huge Pilates area, cycling, running and rowing machines – everything you need to keep fit. There's also a pool, where injured dancers do pool barre and reconditioning work.

I suffered a really severe injury, and all the ligaments in my foot had to be reconstructed. As Kim said, the surgeon you go to will say, "You may not be able to dance again but, you know, you'll be able to walk." For a professional ballet dancer to hear that is soul-destroying. I was put in a cast for six weeks, but luckily because I had the Jerwood Centre, I danced again. Without that support system, I wouldn't have the mobility in my ankle to continue.

...

ANNE: Did the other dancers embrace the Jerwood Centre facilities?

...

CAROL ANNE: It is used every day. It's the dancers' responsibility to keep themselves in shape, though you can't pigeon-hole their approaches. Some dancers love Pilates to stay in condition, although it doesn't do anything for me personally. I work out and exercise on my own – I tend to run and to use the pool to do more aerobic exercise.

...

ANNE: The question of who's responsible for dancers' health and wellbeing is a key one. Mark, do you see a greater sense of responsibility towards the health and wellbeing issues on the part of companies such as Harlequin, who provide goods and services to the dance world?

...

MARK: I'd love to say that there are lots of companies standing shoulder to shoulder with us, saying, "Let's give something back to our customers." But it's a tough world out there and economies are suffering. There's consequently a debate about how far a commercial company is responsible for the wellbeing of its customers. Obviously within a commercial situation everybody has a legal right to be assured that the goods and services they buy are fit for purpose. But how far you go beyond that and support the industry that you work in is something that is down to the DNA of the company concerned.

Our founder, who's still very active in the business, and all the senior managers within Harlequin are passionate about healthy dance practice, but there's only so much you can do alone. I recently met with a company which provides products to dancers, but so far they haven't committed money to any of the programmes that we are sponsoring. The attitude was, "Well, come on, dancers get injured anyway. You know, if you're going to be involved in dance, you're going to get injured." That's frustrating given the good practices that are promoted through Dance UK's Healthier Dance Programme. Dance can be a healthier profession. I just wish that more commercial companies were more committed to that view.
…

ANNE: Erin, in your experience is awareness and support for wellbeing increasing on the part of company directors and management, as well as among the dancers themselves?
…

ERIN: I would say so. At our last Healthier Dancer conference, we had a group of artistic directors from some of the largest ballet companies in the UK and what they said basically was they wanted dancers who could dance for a long time. They don't want dancers who are stick thin, they don't want dancers who are likely to be ill or injured. The issue that they come up against is a financial one, but I also think that dancers need to be imbued with the knowledge that they are not disposable, and that each of them should get the care that they need to be not only excellent performers, but healthy, happy human beings.
…

ANNE: We've been speaking about injuries in the broad sense. Matthew, which specific dance injuries or health issues do you see as most prevalent?
…

MATTHEW: Overtraining and the chronic injuries it causes. Dancers are often pushed to do more, when training is really a question of quality, not quantity. Sometimes companies have a cunning way of saying, "Company class is not part of your contract. Your contract is the rehearsal time, but we expect you to do company class." So they've actually tagged on an extra hour and a half of dancing a day. On top of that, supplemental training often has to be done outside of a dancer's normal working hours. In professional sport, in contrast, the club will look after their players in every aspect, even food. Dancers on tour come out of the theatre and it's often like a wasteland, and they have to travel miles to find somewhere to eat. If that had been a sports club, food would have been put on to help with recovery for the next day.

…

ANNE: You touched upon the difficulty for dancers of finding the time for the additional training they may need. Kim and Carol Anne, is technique class in your view enough to stay fit?

…

CAROL ANNE: For some dancers, yes, but I've found that the older I get, the more I've had to do. At eighteen years old, I could do class, feel totally warm, do a full day of work and not feel any pain. But your body wears down – you need to do more and you need more recovery time, and that means your day gets longer. I would start at about eight o'clock in the morning and do what I needed to do before class, and then do class and then do what I needed to do afterwards. But that's just what we do.

…

KIM: Yes, it can be difficult. I've personally never thought only having a technical class would set you up for the day – it may improve your technical finesse but it wouldn't make you an all-round stronger dancer. I've been drilled from an early age to do alternative training to enhance and strengthen your body. When you work with different choreographers, especially now when dancers may do a Kenneth MacMillan piece and then work with Wayne MacGregor, you need to be versatile enough for whatever gets thrown at you.

…

ANNE: We've discussed the injuries and risks that dancers face, but it's also important to note the positive aspects of being a professional dancer. What beneficial models of behaviour or attitudes can the lifestyle of professional dancers offer to non-professionals?

…

CAROL ANNE: Professional dancers are highly motivated and very self-disciplined, and I think that's why they excel. That's important for anyone who wants to achieve something – you need to have that focus.

…

ERIN: Robert Cohen said during his conference presentation that when a dancer enjoys that moment of absolute concentration, you can feel it as an audience member. In psychology that's called 'flow', the moment at which everything else falls away and you're completely in your body and you're just in the work, feeling the pleasure of it. I think dancers excel at making that a skill, it's not just something that happens by luck, they figure out how to make it happen each day, each performance, so that they can communicate their emotions and joy. And that's something that I think professional dancers could very easily go out and teach to people in the regular world.

…

ANNE: We've got time for a few questions from the audience.

…

AUDIENCE MEMBER #1: Are choreographers desensitised to the risks dancers may unnecessarily take in learning new work?

…

MATTHEW: I think that some choreography has gone to such extremes that we're experiencing the forces you would have on a rugby field. Bodies need time to adapt and they're often not given enough time to prepare for new choreography. Sudden change means stress, and we often see problems when someone has to learn a role too quickly.

...

AUDIENCE MEMBER #2: Carol Anne and Kim, do dancers think about the long-term consequences of the wear and tear on their bodies, or do they tend to think in the short-term?

...

CAROL ANNE: For most of my career, I always thought in that moment. But in the last few years, I thought, "I'm going to retire, oh my goodness, what is my body going to be like? I'm going to be an absolute wreck because I'm so hard on my body." But I think dancers for the most part just think, "I just want to dance." They work so hard to get there, they don't care about what they're going to be like when they're sixty-five.

...

KIM: It becomes almost like a drug. The next moment on stage is more important than your wellbeing at the end of the day, which is hardly ideal, but it's often the brutal truth.

...

ERIN: Medical professionals need to understand that they're talking to someone who's very focused on one thing, one performance, and that they need to help dancers be aware that there are long-term consequences they are going to need to think about. There also needs to be a psychological change in the way that teachers and choreographers and leaders think and how they communicate with those dancers. Because, yes, it is the dancer's responsibility to take care of themselves, but as we discussed, the leaders in those situations need to be aware that the demands that they place on dancers will have lifelong consequences.

...

MARK: I meet a lot of artistic directors and physios as part of my work, and I'm finding that the mentality is beginning to change worldwide. Newer artistic directors may only recently have recovered from injury themselves, and the physios they employ try to educate dancers by saying, "Look, you can dance on this injury now or you can take two weeks off and you won't have to take two months off next year."

...

ANNE: You've touched upon a lot of change, much of it positive, in working towards a better context for professional dancers' health and wellbeing. Thank you all for participating and for the insights you have shared.

Dance, Ageing and Longevity

EDITED BY DR VICTORIA WATTS, LECTURER IN ARTS EDUCATION AT THE UNIVERSITY OF SOUTH AUSTRALIA, PANEL CHAIR

PANELISTS:

Diane Amans: *founder of Freedom in Dance*
Sheila Dickie: *member of Company of Elders*
Clare Guss-West: *Specialist Teacher Trainer on the RAD's Dance for Lifelong Wellbeing research and community outreach project*
Mira Kaushik OBE: *Director of Akademi*

...

VICTORIA: I've asked each of our panelists to talk about their connection to the practice of dance with older learners. I think we can all imagine that there are great numbers of intersections between their various practices, but also probably some areas of difference. Sheila, how did you first become involved in working with older dancers?

...

SHEILA: In 1995, I got a job at Sadler's Wells as the education officer, and part of my role was to look after this group of older people called, in those days, the Lilian Baylis Over-60s Performance Group. It just slipped off the tongue! Anyway, I went to meet them. I thought, "What a nice group of people!" Then I realised how formidable they were. They were all women, twenty-four women, and to them

I was never going to be as good as the person who had been in the job before me, so it took me quite a long time to get used to them. They were all individuals and that's what really struck me, coming from a ballet background where you're all trying to look the same and all aiming for the same thing. This group of people had quite strong personalities, which was evident on stage as well.

The first week I started at Sadler's Wells, a television company was filming them. Suddenly they were all stars. It was quite difficult getting them all into the dressing room, they were all so important. Everybody in Islington recognised them, and they said, "Oh, we want to be treated like professional dancers now." They'd never had dance training – that was part of the remit of this company. And I guess it was quite difficult for them to understand how dancers relate to choreographers. They would start arguing with quite famous choreographers. And I'd be standing, cringing, thinking, "You just don't do that." But they didn't know, so that's the way they behaved, and sometimes they actually had choreographers in tears. I'm

Photos credit Robert Griffin.

not joking! There was one day I went in, it was a Sunday rehearsal, and this well-known choreographer came out and sort of cried on my shoulder and said, "I've never been spoken to like this before." I said, "Well that's just the way they are. Go back in, it will be fine." And everything worked out in the end.

We were talking about dementia earlier in the day and I was thinking back, all the years I've been involved with it, nearly twenty years, nobody in the company has had dementia. People have left to move away from London. They've had various injuries and one thing or another, but not one person has had memory problems. Having said that, none of us can remember from one week to the next what we did!

…

DIANE: I will begin with just a little journey through my dance life and how I started working with older people. I'd been a primary school teacher, was teaching at a college, and alongside that I'd always had a life in dance. In the 1980s I thought, "I've worked with children, I've worked with young people, and I've worked with adults about my age. I'm in my thirties, but I've never worked with older people." Around that time I lost my grandparents – leaving a sort of older-people-sized gap in my life – so I started setting up some opportunities to dance with older people. I approached a local hospital, and I did a project which consisted of weekly sessions, with them taking along some of my students and finishing with a tea dance. I was very nervous about doing that because

I was worried about whether I'd pitch it right, whether I'd sound a bit patronising, and wondering if they'd want to do the kind of activities I'd dreamed up. At a similar time I'd also got a small community grant to work with older people. I had a free venue in the local theatre, so, I was ready to go. Could I get anybody to play? No. I went to residential settings – "What do you mean? What sort of dance? Oh, no, I don't think so, love. No, when you get to my age, no." This went on for a few weeks. I'd got people who wanted to work with me as volunteers and I was all excited about it. In the end I just went around again to a few day centres and residential homes, but I didn't mention the 'D' word. I just invited them for free afternoon tea with homemade cakes and snuck the dance in later.

...

SHEILA: Cake, they always like cake!

...

DIANE: So, following the success of those projects, I put a lottery bid in and got a nice package of money to do some projects. This was in the 90s. I wanted to do project work in community settings – performance work that challenged stereotypes of ageing, not the kind of stuff that perhaps people were expecting – and also some training and continuing professional development for people who wanted to deliver this work.

The first thing I did with this lottery money was devise a roadshow. We took this roadshow around to people in the arts world and also to people involved in delivering services for older people. We demonstrated a little seated dance session – a bit of getting up but mostly seated – and then I asked attendees to fill in a questionnaire at the end that asked whether or not they would like to offer either a space or some money, if they would like their staff to get involved and if they'd like us to do something at their centre. At the end of the first one someone came up and said, "We'd like some. In Bolton. I'd like to do it once a week in four different residential homes." Well I hadn't got the staff to deliver that. I was working full-time in a college and just squeezing this all in extra. So that was when the dance teacher training got fast-forwarded.

Around that time Fergus (Early) and I were meeting with a few others about recognising the need for people to have some kind of specialist continuing professional development in this area. Nowadays I am mostly involved in delivering CPD either with dance artists or with activity leaders. I've just done a project with dance practitioners who are working with people living with dementia, looking at non-verbal ways of facilitating dance. You know, it's one of life's mysteries why dancers talk so much when delivering dance classes!

That's a flavour of what I'm doing now. I have various issues, certain tension lines I see, which we can perhaps come back to later on?

...

VICTORIA: Sure. Clare, I wonder, can you talk about your connection?

...

CLARE: I'm sitting here mainly because of my involvement in mentoring/teaching the teachers who went out on placement for the RAD's Dance and Lifelong Wellbeing initiative. Vicki has asked us to talk about how we got involved working with older people. It's a difficult question because life takes so many unexpected turns. How the heck did I get here?

I was an independent professional dancer and choreographer who then got seriously injured, ignored it, did all the things we all are saying we shouldn't be doing, before finally being diagnosed with the joints of a sixty year-old. I got all the wrong advice, did nothing, deteriorated rapidly, found myself as an honorary octogenarian, and realised that the only way I was going to get through this was by using my own resources. I was lucky enough to still be working at the Opera House here in London as a choreographer, but my own physical state was not good. I had certainly stopped thinking of myself as a dancer. That led to an 'inner journey' so to speak and to cut a long story short I became fascinated with the journey of healing. That was really the start of this.

We've got a lot of community work represented here today but I'm really on the commercial end of services offered to older people. I was asked by Saga and Thomson Holiday's, Thomson Gold, to create a wellbeing animation programme. Now, I had Diane's problem too, really, which is that we started with a pilot programme mostly just delivered by myself so we could put our toe in the water. And then the next thing the companies said was, "Well, we need about sixty of you to deliver it. Can you do it?" And that became

the most joyous experience because I then had to train and also quality assure about sixty 'wellbeing hosts'. For the most part they were dancers and dance teachers working with me on the notion of holistic animation.

Last year was UNESCO's year for active ageing, and I have to say everybody, every institution that I had any dealing with, suddenly wanted programming for the elderly, and were asking me if I could do it. "Clare, could you create an introductory training day?" Or, "Could you deliver something for creative learning managers of all the European opera houses?" Or, "Could you…?" So last year was very busy with formulating this subject for organisations like the RAD, for the International Association of Dance Medicine and Science (IADMS), for the European Network for Opera and Dance Education. I have been training trainers to be able to deliver this kind of work in a way that is safe but also entertaining because the social aspect of those sessions are just as healing as the actual content. Your intention as you go into a session like that, in other words, is just as healing as the content or the knowledge itself, in my personal opinion.

…

VICTORIA: Mira, you can tell us something about your work now?

…

MIRA: I'm not a dancer. I come from theatre and I started working in dance about twenty-five years ago when I became Director of Akademi. When I arrived there I found it very elitist. It was a classical Indian dance organisation based in London, dealing with classical artists creating productions. I was lost. So I had to turn to my community setting of Greenwich, where I worked. I remembered that one of my female friends from my previous job had moved into an old people's home. I went to see her and asked if I could do something for the residents there. I went out, raised funds, and within six months got a project started in this community group. I sent in a dancer to start working with residents using very soft art forms: some dance, some Tai Chi and so on. And it worked fabulously. But by the end of the six months my dancer was carrying bags of shopping for everybody who lived there. So, the question was, were we dancing or were we performing a social service? That's where the discussion started.

Within that year I went to Holloway Prison to meet some older Asian women and I discovered that they were very isolated. They had no means to communicate with the outer world: they were abandoned. They were all there for drug trafficking and the world had disappeared for them. By the time I got the funds raised to go and see these women in the remand prison, they had all moved on and instead I had a whole bunch of women from Africa. They were incredibly demanding about what they wanted to do from Indian cinema – so we had this mad project with older women doing Bollywood. And from then on, working with older people became intrinsic to Akademi.

Older Asian people often think it's frivolous to dance and are very embarrassed about expending anything on physicality. At the same time, we never age in south Asian dance. My seventy-year-old dancers who are now going to participate in the production I'm planning for next year – I've got about thirty-five of them – are a fabulous set of people. They don't believe that they have aged, but that the community matures and gets better with time. They don't realise the reality of their age and they carry on moving. But their perception means that they perform like sixteen-year-olds. They believe that they are sixteen-year-old dancers – young women and men – which is beautiful and hilarious as well!

. . .

VICTORIA: There are so many points of connection here. I've got a list to do with identity and agency and workforce development and how we engage learners and what are the barriers to participation, and on and on. But rather than me posing a question to all of you, I'm going to let you now pick a topic that one of the others spoke about and ask you to respond to that.

. . .

CLARE: I'd love at some point to get on to longevity. It's such a key thing in our society at the moment and none of us actually touched on it yet. We talked about age but not actually on longevity, so, do you want me to launch the subject?

. . .

VICTORIA: Go ahead, please do.

. . .

CLARE: We know that one in four people alive today will live to be over a hundred: in part because of improvements in medical science we have greater prospects for longevity. But that doesn't tell us anything about the quality of that extended life. Most of us don't want to live that extended life if it's going to be with pain, with dependency, with depression, with isolation, and so forth. So I've been working a lot with 'life enhancement and longevity' programmes, because the reality of people living to well over a hundred with perhaps all the concerns I just mentioned is not necessarily good news. For me, dance has got an essential role to play here.

…

VICTORIA: That connects very strongly to what Sheila was saying about her company members, in terms of their wellbeing.

…

SHEILA: It's the pleasure they get from it, the social interaction, the friendships they make. I think Company of Elders might be a bit different because it's very much geared to performance, not just coming and doing a class each week which, again, is very beneficial. Our outreach classes also have performance elements since I saw what that did to people. When they rehearsed together, they've gone wrong, they've fallen out with each other, and then they've got it right and they have a wonderful performance, they're all on a high. And that re-energises them, and they don't seem to get any older. It's amazing.

…

MIRA: I've been based in Camden Town for the last twenty-five years. The women who are participating in our older women's project now, I've seen as young mothers. In the late eighties

they were not allowed out. They lived locally in these council estates, and they prevented their daughters from participating in our youth projects. Slowly I've seen them grow more confident, more mature, until now, twenty years later; they are finally taking part in our projects. Longevity is about what is happening in your head as well as in the body.

…

DIANE: If I can just segue into one thing here, I think it really is important to get under the skin of what dance can offer, as far as healthy ageing goes, but the tension line for me is that it is an art form and I don't want it to always be promoted as part of a healthy ageing programme, a falls prevention programme, and so on and so forth. I'm not above taking your money for that but I'll always be clear – I'm aiming to make art. Okay? Look, quite often it is exercise by stealth: people will come to dance where they perhaps find the seated exercise a bit boring. But that's a tension line for me. Those funding opportunities and making sure we're clear as artists that this is still an art form and we are making art.

…

VICTORIA: We had lots of conversations about that topic on the Dance for Lifelong Wellbeing project. We're not therapists, but actually it's about the artistry of dance and giving people an opportunity to find that joy, that playfulness…

…

DIANE: Yes, it's the joy thing. Another thing is the language of burden which often accompanies talk about us getting older. The statistics you've mentioned [to Clare] are usually accompanied by some language of burden about the 'problem of getting older' and 'how we are going to pay for all these older people'. I'm really keen for any opportunity to challenge stereotypes so that older people are not seen as somehow draining the country of resources.

...

VICTORIA: Would anyone in the audience like to jump in?

...

AUDIENCE MEMBER #1: When I spoke with some of the older women who took part in the Dance for Lifelong Wellbeing sessions they all said to me, "Oh, but I used to dance. Tommy and I used to go..." and this lovely life story would come out.

...

AUDIENCE MEMBER #2: My mum's ageing and has dementia. She used to dance, you know, when she was young. They all danced much more than my generation.

...

SHEILA: I notice with the Company of Elders that they were all expert at ballroom. They could all waltz, quickstep and tango. When it comes to my generation, we were the baby boomers. A lot of us had done ballet as children, or we'd had dance in schools, so people still went back to that. They may have only done it for a few years, but they were still quite happy to come back, and it's just a different style, a different way of moving.

...

MIRA: In the world of Indian dance, expression work is very important and is done by more mature artists. Over the years I've been gathering all these ageing dancers and asking them to work on their creative expression. This has filtered through to such an extent that this year's annual British Dance Edition (taking place in Edinburgh) is going to have a dancer, who's over sixty, representing British dance. It's very unusual for an ageing performer to be pitching for an international tour. She just happened to be an Indian dancer in this country. So I feel very hopeful and very positive.

...

VICTORIA: I think our discussion as a whole has highlighted that sort of hope and optimism, by dispelling some misperceptions about older dancers. Thank you for sharing your insights on some of the unexpected benefits of staying active in later life.

Enriching Young Lives: Dance and Personal Development

EDITED BY MICHELLE GROVES, DEAN OF THE FACULTY OF EDUCATION AT THE ROYAL ACADEMY OF DANCE, PANEL CHAIR

PANELISTS:
Robert Parker: *Artistic Director,*
Elmhurst School for Dance
Rob Lynden: *Artistic Director, Dance United*
Rhian Robbins: *Independent Dance Artist*
Fergus Early OBE: *Artistic Director,*
Green Candle Dance Company

...

MICHELLE: Our panel will consider the effect of dance on young people, from training, career development and education, to dance programmes for minority and inter-generational groups. Robert, perhaps you can set the conversation rolling by telling us how vocational dance training has changed since you were a student?

...

ROBERT: Having retired fairly recently from Birmingham Royal Ballet, I remember clearly what my own training was like, so I can obviously draw comparisons to what I'm seeing in Elmhurst at the moment. Through conversations with Kevin O'Hare (Artistic Director, Royal Ballet) and Christopher Hampson (Artistic Director, Scottish Ballet),

and as someone who has just stepped out of the industry myself, I feel I can judge what dance companies actually want to see of the young talent coming out of the schools.

It's probably safe to say that training methods have changed dramatically with regard to discipline. Today, dance teachers promote positive discipline in the classroom, whereas when I was a student I can recall instances of students being pulled by their hair, having fingernails scratched down backs to get shoulder blades down, or a lit cigarette held under a knee in a *développé à la seconde.* Hopefully those days are behind us, given our greater awareness of safeguarding. As dance teachers we have a responsibility to look after the welfare of students and produce well-rounded human beings. Concentrating on the individual is definitely different to what it used to be.

Today we are more aware of sports science and psychology. There is just so much we can be learning from the sport sector and it's great to be bringing this knowledge into dance. At Elmhurst we have thorough screenings of our

Opposite: Elmhurst School for Dance students waiting in the wings during a Birmingham Royal Ballet rehearsal of *Cinderella.* Photo credit Andrew Ross.

students to flag up any potential issues to be aware of. We are also drawing on research coming out of the National Institute of Dance Medicine and Science and Dance UK and forging links with other institutions.

…

MICHELLE: Do you think that dance teachers who have followed a tradition of 'this is how we teach ballet' are adapting their teaching, or ways of thinking about teaching, to fit in with the developments you have mentioned?

…

ROBERT: I think so, because the industry as a whole is changing. The demands of choreographers are changing. Everything is much more international. Dancers today have to be versatile. They have to go from performing *Sleeping Beauty* or *Swan Lake* one evening to a mixed triple bill of modern choreography the next. Dancers' bodies need to be adequately prepared for that, and it's something that I actively promote with the students at Elmhurst. I want to target a 'holistic' approach to fitness, including bringing in more aerobic fitness – swimming, running – even sports such as netball and tennis. We're thinking of introducing enrichment activities where students can learn about team playing to give them leadership skills. It's really about trying to enrich students as human beings and to give them transferable skills that will carry on long after their dance careers finish. Artistic Directors are wanting more autonomy in dancers so that when they join a company they're already free-thinking individuals,

willing to get their hands dirty, to have choreographic input and not just stand there saying, "Yes, sir, no sir, three bags full sir!" Those days are gone.

…

MICHELLE: Not all of the students at Elmhurst will go on to a professional career, and some may have relatively short careers. What do you feel is your responsibility as artistic director in preparing students for life outside the dance world?

…

ROBERT: Like you say, not every student is going to make it as a professional dancer. At Elmhurst we try to treat students as young adults. If you don't patronise or act in a condescending manner towards them they will act like adults. It's that old adage: if you treat someone like a child, they may as well act like a child, but treat them like adults and they'll meet you halfway. We have to guide and support students in becoming self-sufficient. For example, if a teacher is ill one day and there isn't a teacher to cover, let's say, a lesson in solo performance, what's to stop the students actually delivering the lesson themselves? One student can lead, they can correct each other – it's all about student-directed learning.

Changing the ethos and mentality of some teachers can be challenging, but they have to move with the times. I've introduced iPads into the classroom which are great teaching aids for things like understanding anatomy or filming students and playing it back to them. Some teachers can't even swipe the 'on' button, but they are learning. We all have to be adaptive as the world is changing.

…

MICHELLE: Rob, tell us about Dance United and how you think dance can transform lives, particularly for young people who are marginalised in society?

…

ROB: I was interested to note the word 'enrichment' in the title of this session. Dance United works with young people who, for the most part, are on the margins. They will be disengaged, out of mainstream education, and very often known to youth offending teams. They will be known to people in referral units or other organisations which deal with people who have failed in mainstream education contexts. It's not necessarily about enrichment – it's about engagement. What Dance United does quite distinctively is work with individuals over a considerable period of time. Ten weeks is the standard provision; every day between ten o'clock and four o'clock. For some, just completing one or two days is a real achievement. Generally we work with about twenty young people who have been referred to us by youth offending services.

At the heart of what we do is working up to a dance performance in front of friends, family and referral partners. Working towards the performance is a key achievement for many of the participants. It gives young people a huge feeling of having accomplished something, very often for the first time in a very long time. Our aim is to produce a high quality,

professional performance, and we work with professional choreographers and other production professionals.

Imagine stepping into a classroom for the first time with a group of six fifteen-year-old girls who are out of mainstream education, with a lot of issues, with a lot of street-wise knowledge and normally not too good at being quiet and listening to things.

Then, imagine throwing into the mix three 19 year-old boys along with some older people – 22-25 year-olds. Instantly you've got a dynamic on your hands. The mix is important because it's about getting a balance. It's about young people being able to see what they may become in three years' time. Getting those

Above: Dance United in performance. Photo credit Pari Naderi courtesy of Dance United.

young people to be still, to stand in parallel, to be spatially aware, to look at everybody, to listen to what is being asked of them, and to focus on the job that they've got to do, are great achievements. Often they have come from extremely chaotic backgrounds, the sort of backgrounds that we can't even begin to imagine. Some of our provision is in Kings Cross, London, which is what we refer to as a 'postcode neutral' area. They come, they're in a safe environment, they get into a class, and the doors are closed. They might have issues with just about everyone around them and everything that's going on, but once they realise that those issues can be dealt with they begin to focus on the important thing: dance.

Dance United won't ever put a young person out on a stage if we think they are not going to look their absolute best. Standards have to be high. We don't audition or discriminate on grounds of ability. It's important that everybody has their moment. That might just be walking across the stage at the start or during part of the choreography. But everybody must have their moment.

...

MICHELLE: Can you tell us about one or two of your success stories?

...

ROB: There are countless success stories. We primarily operate out of London but we started the project in Yorkshire where we found very supportive partners in the Youth Offending team up there. We've also got a project in Winchester. Overall, the programme has shown to cut re-offending by 66%, with 88%

of the participants returning to education, employment or training. The personal stories are always really rather lovely because what you often see is kids who start off being incredibly offensive a lot of the time; they're in your face. But when they feel they're in a safe environment they get to know themselves as individuals, to take chances and re-engage with the world.

...

MICHELLE: What is it about dance that makes the difference? Wouldn't drama or music fulfil the same role?

...

ROB: We work with contemporary dance to create a very democratic environment. You say to potential participants, "You're coming to do contemporary dance," and they have no idea what you're talking about. They all come in on an equal basis. If we were to do street dance, there would be bound to be somebody who has a better outfit for it, knows the moves or has a better look. Dance is about 'embodied confidence'. I don't know that music or drama gives you that. This is what some of the young people have had to say:

"The way I am creating and expressing meaning through the dance demonstrates that I can make some sense of my life and I can be more in control of the choices I make."

"I am here without my normal props, barefoot even, totally exposed and nowhere to hide. This communicates my self-confidence."

"The new (and significantly challenging) dance techniques I have learnt demonstrate that I can push myself beyond what I think I am capable of, take some risks and achieve."

"'My moments of stillness and focus within the dance show how far I can feel comfortable with myself and hold on to something inside me when the going gets tough."

"Dancing as part of a group communicates how well I can work with other people and that I am trusted. The highly professional nature of the production in which I performed communicates that I equally value myself."

"The way you applaud at the end of the performance signals to me that I am visible, acknowledged and appreciated."

...

MICHELLE: Rhian, as a freelance dance artist and teacher you must come across a range of different learners. What are some of the similarities and differences between these different groups?

...

RHIAN: I work across a range of projects and some of these might well involve students who have ambitions to become professional dancers. I also work with young people who have just been introduced to dance or may be discovering dance for the first time, and not just as an 'extracurricular' activity. With some of the projects I am involved in the students don't have a choice. We arrive, we choose them, and eventually we hope they'll choose us. So yes, a huge range of learners. Seeing shared feelings, the motivation, passion and connection with dance is incredibly exciting. Like Rob said, you want them to have a reason to get out of bed. It's a reason to go to school because that's the day that they will have dance and they'll feel good about it. It gives them a sense of worth.

In one of the projects I'm involved with, I visit primary schools, teaching ballet in a creative way to a single class. Selected children are then invited to attend additional ballet classes within the community. We identify children who have a real curiosity and engagement with dance, those who want to learn over and above what happens in the weekly workshop. That raw energy – that hunger – is something that we want to see and instil in students. I guess it's then a question of sustaining it – can that be tapped, can it be developed and will it continue into full-time training?

A number of years ago dance in education in the UK was on the march. The dots were beginning to be joined up between dance providers and dance organisations. In response to this is a project that I am involved in, run by the Royal Ballet School's Partnership and Access programme. Royal Ballet School Students work collaboratively with students in a local state school. Over a six month period, both sets of students came together, visiting each other's schools to work on a joint choreographic project. The state school students had certain perceptions of the Royal Ballet School students but eventually realised the two groups had a lot in common. Equally,

Above: A Green Candle
Dance Session

the Royal Ballet students were a bit scared about going into a big comprehensive school. The most precious thing that I brought away from that project was how the two groups of teenagers had so many similarities and how differences were transcended through working creatively with each other. There was a sort of fusion and a great respect between them. I guess the best outcome for a project such as this is for somebody to say, "Oh my goodness, I didn't know which dancer was from which group!"

…

MICHELLE: Do you feel your approaches to teaching and your expectations differ depending on what type of student group you are working with?

…

RHIAN: Adaptability is of the essence. There's no single, blanket approach. It's important that we consider all the students we teach and realise that they are individual learners and they will learn in different ways. I am looking to do more than teach them to dance. We need to develop self-sufficient students, self-sustaining artists, individual human beings who will be able to work and respond positively to different social environments.

…

MICHELLE: Fergus, as well as working with older people, Green Candle Dance Company works with younger people in a relatively deprived area of London which has a large ethnic minority population. Has the Company's work helped with social integration and understanding of identity for this group?

...

FERGUS: Well, one hopes. It's fairly impossible to measure. We have a group in Mulberry School for Girls in Bethnal Green which is called 'Bangla-hop'. Roughly speaking, it's a kind of a Bangla-street/contemporary fusion. They are superb dancers, beautiful dancers, incredibly focused and incredibly motivated. But there's great difficulty in finding opportunities for them to perform. It's not something that's sanctioned very much by their families or by their culture in general. We can only get them in a position to perform their work if it is a school-sanctioned event. We can't say, "Oh we're going to have them in our show here and there." All of us are breaking down barriers in all sorts of ways, but I wouldn't like to make too heavy a claim.

...

MICHELLE: Green Candle Dance Company has some inter-generational projects. What has been the impact of younger dancers working with older dancers and vice versa?

...

FERGUS: This is one of the areas that I think is most effective in terms of social connection. Some of the best outcomes from a successful inter-generational project are comments like, "I didn't know that older people could be fun", or "I didn't know that young people could be so nice!" Generational perceptions are major barriers in our society. Most of our thinking is about dividing society up into bits, and 'young and old' are two of the bits we like to keep

separate. To devise a show together is a wonderful experience. Green Candle will bring our senior dancers together with our youth groups. We give them a chance to have tea and biscuits together – very, very simple.

Recently we created a show for an audience of two to four year-olds and performed it in an older people's day centre, so the audience was made up of children, their parents and older people. We try to find places where we can have community-type shows for all ages, but it's a huge undertaking.

...

MICHELLE: Why do you think it's important for Green Candle to be exposing very young people to dance?

...

FERGUS: Well from our point of view, they're the best audience – a wonderful audience! They're fantastic. Children are wonderful, and it's the early years when you learn and develop most. The show involves a lot of participation with a lot of chances for children to join in. You can almost see them soaking up things. The older children would, not surprisingly, be braver and really get involved. For the performers it was great because every show was a hugely different experience; they didn't know what to expect so they had to be really on their toes. We performed in day centres and nursery schools so the stage area was very small with up to thirty children and their parents and carers sitting very close. With young children, how much noise you make and how big you are can be very frightening, so we had to temper the level of performance according to audience response.

…

MICHELLE: Imagine a world where all participation in dance was banned. What would that world look like, and more specifically, what would be the implications for the social, cultural and personal fulfilment of individuals?

…

ROB: It would be a very sad world. Dance is something that's fundamental. So many people engage with dance in so many different ways. People do it on a basis that we might not recognise in any kind of form or capacity, but I think the world would be a much sadder place without it.

…

RHIAN: It's just not how the world would look: how would it feel, how would it sound, how would it taste? Creative subjects, such as dance, in schools are under threat. We really must ensure creativity is properly valued and continue the fight.

The creative sector has grown four times faster in the UK than any other type of workforce, employing 2.5 million people. That's more than the financial services, advanced manufacturing and construction. It is a growing workforce and one that governments can't ignore.

…

ROBERT: I'm thinking of the movie *Footloose*! If you did outlaw dance, I think there could be some very exciting pockets of resistance. I think it would breed a lot of avant garde creativity. It could be that you'd see some very unique performances going on behind closed doors. Dance is essential, a journey of self-discovery. Dance brings people together, it's a social thing. It's one of the fundamental aspects of living that you can't get rid of.

…

FERGUS: I was trying to imagine such a world but couldn't. It's been tried a couple of times. Cromwell tried, didn't he? The Taliban tried in Afghanistan not so long ago. All you can say about that is, it didn't last very long, which is hopeful.

…

MICHELLE: Indeed! I'd like to thank each of you for bringing a wealth of experience to our discussion about the power of dance to enrich young lives.

Dancing for Our Lives?

EDITED BY MICHELLE GROVES, DEAN, AND DR CAROL MARTIN, DANCE HISTORIAN AND FORMER HEAD OF RESEARCH OF THE FACULTY OF EDUCATION AT THE ROYAL ACADEMY OF DANCE, PANEL CHAIR

PANELISTS:
Jackie Hayhoe: *Age UK*
Linda Jasper: *Director, Youth Dance England*
Dr Victoria Showunmi: *Lecturer in Education, Institute of Education*
Kenneth Olumuyiwa Tharp OBE: *Chief Executive, The Place*
Dr Susan Venn: *Research Fellow and Co-Director of the Centre for Research on Ageing and Gender, University of Surrey*

…

CAROL: Our panel brings together researchers and practitioners whose collective expertise spans a range of initiatives with amateur and professional dances of all ages. Linda, can you begin the discussion by telling us how Youth Dance England has made dance more accessible to young people, and what have been some of the organisation's major achievements?

…

LINDA: I think that Youth Dance England's work and its particular achievements really started to transform when we worked with Tony Hall, who was then Chief Executive of the Royal Opera House, to produce The Dance Review report [2008] which was commissioned by the Labour government. This led to the first ever major investment in children and young people's dance in and beyond school. £5.5 million was awarded to the Arts Council, and Youth Dance England was designated to deliver a national brief. That was a significant milestone. It was the first time that Youth Dance England worked nationally with a model that had been supposedly emulated by other art forms. We worked with existing dance organisations in order to deliver three objectives: to widen access to dance, to raise the quality of dance provision and to improve the progression routes for young people into training for professional careers.

For the first time we had a cohesive framework operational across England. There were nine regional plans, alongside a national plan, through which we devised national programmes such as U.Dance, where youth dance performances take place at county, regional and national levels. This year the

national performance is in Leeds where, for the first time, we'll be taking over four venues. There are so many groups now performing, and we'll have over 600 young people that have been selected through a number of regional performances arriving in Leeds.

Another significant initiative is Young Creatives, where we work with the Royal Ballet School and the Royal Opera House. Young Creatives is a training mentoring programme for young choreographers under the age of 19. We also have a national young dance ambassador's programme, which showcases experiences of young people as performers, creators, viewers, critics and leaders of dance.

As a result of the Arts Council funding, Youth Dance England's initiatives were monitored and evaluated by an independent evaluator, appointed by the Arts Council, who worked with us for three years. At the end of those three years we'd had 390,425 young people participating in all our programmes, 15% of English schools had taken part in new dance performances and over 1,800 performances had taken place in England.

...

CAROL: Kenneth, how has accessibility to vocational training in contemporary dance widened?

...

KENNETH: At The Place we have vocational training; our doors are open to people from a very young age and also to more mature artists like Richard Alston, so we cover the whole gamut. There has been a huge change in terms of widening participation, but this change has not been brought about by The Place alone. We've done it with help from all our colleagues in the sector. In a sense there has been a journey, a very important journey. However someone gets their first taste of dance, it's important that there are routes for them to carry on and progress, whether it is as hobby or going on to vocational training.

Centres for Advanced Training (CATs), which are government funded programmes, not only aim to raise the standards of young people going into vocational training, but they also provide opportunities for young people to have access to high quality training wherever they may be located, regardless of their socio-economic circumstances. I'm so delighted the CATs have been going for so long, and we are really seeing the results. The Place was one of the very first CATs, but now I think there are ten across the country, and that is so important for young people. Quite a lot of young people who go into CATs will come through the youth dance movement. They will come from having their first dance experience either within the school curriculum or in an out-of-school dance club.

It has always been a struggle to get boys into dance. I know at the Royal Ballet School they talked about the Billy Elliot effect, and after the *Billy Elliot* film came out I think they had a year when, for the first time, they offered more places to young boys than girls. Two years ago at The Place, we had 24 male and 26 female new students walk through our doors. In the following year we had almost the same number of males. As a result of CATs,

Opposite: RAD image.

we have seen students coming from wider socio-economic backgrounds, as well as from different dance styles. A lot of young men are coming through the hip-hop route. The Swindon CAT, for example, has an urban dance programme.

...

CAROL: Jackie, how has the 'Fit as a Fiddle' programme offered through Age UK engaged older people in dance?

...

JACKIE: My background was PE and sports, but I'm passionate about dance. I love dance. I go to performances, and I was invited to The Place 33 years ago where I met a young Bob Cohan. It was the most marvelous experience.

Fit as a Fiddle is a project funded by the Big Lottery. It aims to improve the health and wellbeing of older people, and when we say old, normally we go from 65 years of age upwards, but for the purposes of our funding it was 50+ years of age. 25% of our participants are over 85, so that gives you an idea of the 'older old'! So far, 350,000 people have taken part. We run classes and activities all over the country, and dance is one of the activities. We ask people what they want to do. We've had an 86 year-old wanting to do abseiling! We work in residential care homes, and the dance activities have been great fun. It's all about making activities enjoyable.

When people come to Fit as a Fiddle we ask them about themselves and how much activity they do, how much cardiovascular, strength and balance type exercise. The aim of the project was to reach people that needed to become physically fitter. We've had amazing results. Everybody has got fitter, so we know it works. We also ask them about their diet and their wellbeing. If you talk to people at the National Institute for Health and Care Excellence (NICE), they will say physical activity and mental wellbeing are related. We can now prove that. We measure people as they come in, we measure them after they've finished their activities, and we measure them three months later. What we see is a remarkable increase in relation to their mental wellbeing. Many older people feel isolated and lonely, but through Fit as a Fiddle they have a social connectedness, and it's fun.

The dance that we do ranges from belly dancing, which seems very popular, to Zumba and ballroom dancing. The 'Gay Gordons' in Camden is a group of older men who literally dance the Gay Gordon in kilts, and it's great to watch. We have started to look at reminiscence dancing in relation to dementia because it brings out so many different things – our senses, and what is innate in us. When we listen to music we all see or hear something, regardless of whether or not one suffers with dementia. These experiences add value to the quality of life, which is very important as we get older.

Older people love dancing. We have a 96 year-old lady who comes to our tea dances. She wraps her gold dance shoes in crepe paper and brings them along every week. She looks about 70 and has a penchant for the younger men! A 70 year-old man will walk into a class and she will literally shout 'toy boy!' and make her way over. We've now trained her to be a dance buddy. New people will be allocated a dance buddy so they don't feel isolated and lonely. If you are on your own it's a big step to cross the threshold. We encourage people to become dance buddies, and we now have over 100 dance buddies dotted all over the country.

...

CAROL: Are there any similarities with the Fit as a Fiddle programme and what has been observed in the Faculty of Education's Dance and Lifelong Wellbeing project?

...

VICTORIA: I was invited to take part in the Dance and Lifelong Wellbeing project as an independent researcher by the project leader, Dr Victoria Watts. As a result of observing the participants, and in discussion with others working on the project, I devised a research method which I hoped would be able to gather all the voices of the participants, stakeholders and teachers. As a 'traditional academic', I had to throw out my original ideas and think, "Well, how can I make this happen so we do collect the voices in a creative space, and for it to benefit the project?" That was one of the things I observed – the dynamics of the creative space.

I suppose the other thing I observed was how my interpretation of dance matched the interpretations of the teachers and the learners. That was, in itself, like a triangle which I was working with, so I went away with a lot of reflecting to do – reflecting on how what I had observed had influenced me personally, as well as how dance had

influenced my role as a researcher when working with older people.

The analysis of the project's data is ongoing, but we have started to think about the male voice and the female voice and what that means. Throughout the project we have been considering how the project's teachers adapted their approaches to teaching when working with groups where some of the learners were physically challenged while others had more mobility. In relation to some of the points which have already been discussed, I have observed emotional responses such as of happiness and 'buzziness', especially when the learners realised that they were able to move their limbs/joints a little further each time. It's not so much a sense of fitness, more a sense of achievement.

...

CAROL: There is an interesting dynamic between aging and gender. Susan, what can we learn from our observations?

...

SUSAN: As a sociologist I'm always observing what goes on with interaction. The first thing that came to me is that a lot of us feel the need to share that we are non-dancers, or dancers, and I think that is quite interesting because my children will say I'm a non-dancer. But, because I dance round the kitchen, I actually think I am a dancer! So I think it's a mistake for us to say we are non-dancers or non-singers.

The Centre for Research on Ageing and Gender is actually a virtual centre, so there are only two or three of us sharing a small office. We have done lots of pioneering work which has explored various issues around inequality, particularly around older people and trying to get recognition that older people are actually a heterogeneous group. It is very tempting to lump older people all together as one group, but if you think about it, we have talked about an age range of 50 to 96 years of age. That is a 46-year span, and within this span is an awful lot of variety. 'Older' people are just people who happen to be going through life and getting older.

We've also conducted some pioneering work which looks at older women and gender inequalities, raising issues around pensions and all that kind of serious stuff. It's also worth mentioning that men are often neglected when it comes to research, and that has come out as an issue in this panel discussion. It's important to make sure that men's own particular needs are also recognised.

I love multi-disciplinary work and working with creative disciplines, probably because I came very late into my discipline of sociology. I worked for a long while with an artist who did installations about sleep, which led to the point of letting her film me all night long with the lights on! We've talked about creativity; I think we can get so locked in to our disciplines that we lose that broader notion of creativity. Interestingly, the best work I've done and the best that has come out of that work has been with people who seem to be diametrically opposed to where I'm coming from. So, I get on brilliantly with bio-medical engineers, with artists, with designers because they are open-minded.

We've talked about youth and we've talked about older people. We've talked at different ends of the spectrum, and we tend to problematise those areas. Youths are seen as being problematic, but so are older people, particularly my group; the 'baby boomers'. My view is that inter-generational research is a really good way to demystify some of the misconceptions, and I can see lots of areas where this could happen, for example, young people working together with older people, or young dancers working with older dancers. I was involved with a small project where young nurses worked with older people to co-create a radio play that explored tensions and misperceptions about each group. It wasn't just the play itself that was brilliant, the entire process was.

It's hugely important to me that men are not left out of all of this, despite their apparent reluctance to engage in any type of research project. We know that older men are much more likely to be lonely. They don't go to day centres because they are full of older women. Older women are much more social. In terms of lifelong learning, if we can capture men and boys early on, this could carry them through into much later on in their life course. Sociologists have done work on athletes and ballet dancers in terms of how they perceive their ageing bodies, and whether that impacts on their own identity, and I think that would also be a useful avenue to explore further.
…

LINDA: For youth dance, gender in relation to health and wellbeing is always a double-edged sword. On the one hand the Department of Health is very interested in dance as a way of getting girls and young women active and, to be frank, a lot of civil servants are only interested in this aspect as an argument to fund dance at all. On the other hand we all want equal opportunities for boys as well as girls to take part in dance. If the proposals for dance within the revised National Curriculum for England go ahead, there is a possibility that dance will be embedded within Physical Education at Key Stage 3. That would mean that boys would have an entitlement to dance.

The dance workforce is very female-dominated. However, we want equal opportunities. How we actually deliver dance to young people is often in single sex groups. We are finding that in youth dance we have a proliferation of boys only dance groups. Such groups have become very popular. However, in terms of making political arguments, we come unstuck. We see the benefit of dance for all, but our political masters, most of whom are male, actually want dance for girls.

. . .

KENNETH: I wanted to pick up on the point made about inter-generational projects. At least two of our Work Place associate artists have been developing their practice very intensely in a number of inter-generational projects. Two years ago in Barcelona I saw one of the dance pieces one of the artists had created. There was a cast of 120 dancers, six of whom were professional artists, with the rest of the group ranging from parents and toddlers right the way through to older people.

Photo credit Robert Griffin.

I turned up at the end of the project, and the tangible bond between those people was so powerful. It was a bond which will be sustained way after the project. I suppose I'm just reflecting that there aren't many opportunities where people of very different ages can easily, comfortably, naturally come together and share something without feeling awkward. I'm not saying inter-generational work is easy, but I think there is something incredibly powerful about such projects, there is almost a societal need for that sense of community.

. . .

CAROL: There certainly is. Thank you all for exploring the diverse ways that dance can transcend social barriers and nurture inter-generational communities.

PART TWO

PROJECTS
PROFILES
PERSPECTIVES

Gillian Lynne: 'Disturbing the Air'

BY DAVID JAYS

Even when feeling ill, anxious and decidedly wobbly, Gillian Lynne can hold an audience in the palm of her hand. Her keynote address to the RAD Faculty of Education conference on Dance for Lifelong Wellbeing came as she was recovering from a severe bout of pneumonia. "It's not pretty being 87," she announced, "so it is essential to have a purpose – a reason to work and to keep at it." Even in illness, she explained, her indefatigable work ethic kicked in, together with lessons from a career in conjuring pizzazz from thin air. "Straighten up the neck and fire the nipples!" she told herself. It worked.

The conference heralded a series of honours marking a career in dance that has taken Lynne from the formative days of British ballet to the growth of the 'megamusical'. Two days after the RAD address, she received a lifetime achievement award at the Olivier Awards. She was still weak – "It's a long job, pneumonia. They told me it usually kills people in their eighties" – but she was sustained by a sense of responsibility to an audience and the gratifying sense that, in her ninth decade, she's still in the game. "I thought, if I'm going to die as a result of this, it had better be a good speech. I went on for ten minutes."

Yet more gratifyingly, in early 2014 she was appointed a Dame of the British Empire. "I'm not the sort of person who would ever become a dame," she told me, noting that there are 'wonderful ballet dames' – including Beryl Grey, a friend from childhood. The honour acknowledged one of her great achievements: leading British musical theatre from its status as a fey, parochial cousin of Broadway razzle dazzle into an international creative force.

As with many artists, signs of creativity appeared in childhood. When Lynne, born in 1926, was growing up in Kent, her anxious mother took her to the doctor. "They all thought I'd got St Vitus' Dance, because I could not sit still." The doctor, unconvinced, left the child in his consulting room with the radio playing, and then looked through the glass door to find her dancing all over his desk. Describing the scene to me in 2005, Lynne hooted with laughter. "The doctor said, 'For God's sake, get her to dance classes now!'"

Lynne trained in classical ballet under Molly Lake. "She worked with Pavlova for years, she was a wonderful, strict woman.

Opposite: Photo credit Christopher Kennedy, Camera Press London.

Molly's tutoring about pas de deux was incredible, and she taught me *Le Papillion* [by Taglioni], of all the difficult dances." The conjunction 'wonderful, strict' stands out; Lynne has no time for mollycoddling. "They have to go together, or you don't have a hope," she insists. "You need the love and the militant strictness."

Both qualities characterised Ninette de Valois, founder of the Sadler's Wells Ballet, which Lynne joined aged 17, in 1944. Working a field still dominated by male choreographers, producers and artistic directors, Lynne was fortunate to experience this woman's imperturbable drive: "a brilliant choreographer who ran her company with the tenacity of a 10 ton truck." "She was magnificent and inspirational," Lynne said in a BBC documentary. "I would have killed for her, really."

De Valois in turn called Lynne 'the smiler', and this optimism sustained her through the Blitz, with doodlebugs attacking during *Les Sylphides*, and a perilous tour of war-torn Europe. Lynne was part of the company that re-opened the Royal Opera House with *The Sleeping Beauty* in 1946, and left what was then the Royal Ballet five years later.

Her choreographic yen soon emerged. "When people were choreographing for me I used to say that annoying thing – 'Couldn't we do that?' I hate it when people say it to me…" She highlights some early work that receives less attention than her collaborations with Lloyd Webber. The jazz ballet *Collages* premiered at the 1963 Edinburgh Festival. "It changed my life, and I hope it changed the choreographic life of England at that time." She collaborated with Dudley Moore – now best remembered as a comedian and film star, but also an accomplished composer. They became close friends and confidants. "Dudley was having terrible trouble with his love life," she recalls. "He had an excess of females and could never make the right choice, while I could never find the right person."

The collaboration also aided her work. "My timings were influenced by Dudley," she insists. "He showed me how you could play around with rhythm." That gift for the unexpected caught the eye of Broadway producer David Merrick. He came to see *Collages* "in the basement of a church in Edinburgh", but Lynne didn't believe reports of a big cheese in the audience, so "I was sitting talking to my cast in a dirty old dressing gown" when Merrick appeared and announced, "I'll have you on Broadway in a year."

She is also proud of *The Matchgirls* (1966), which she describes as "the first working-class musical." Her first musical as a director, it evoked the 1888 strike over conditions by women working in London match factories. "By the first interval," she recalls, "we got an offer for Broadway. It was really appreciated by the public – it was a very important story."

Lynne had premiered Ashton ballets, sparkled in revue, acted opposite Errol Flynn in *The Master of Ballantrae* and played Puck in a BBC production of *A Midsummer Night's Dream*, but the unforeseen success of *Collages* brought her performing career to a premature close. "I still had all that love for dancing, but I

Opposite: Photo credit Christopher Kennedy, Camera Press London.

was just too busy," she says. Her choreography similarly encompasses classical and modern dance, ballet and musicals, stage and screen. She resents being pigeon-holed ("I think it's insulting"), and received encouragement from pioneering choreographer Martha Graham, who "was wonderful to my little company because she could see what I was trying to do."

Lynne has consistently brought dance to a vast audience – through such musicals as *Cats*, *Phantom of the Opera* and *Chitty Chitty Bang Bang*, the BBC television ballet *A Simple Man* (1987) and films such as *Half a Sixpence* and *Yentl*. Even so, she makes her achievements sound like happenstance piled on accident. Would she describe herself as ambitious? "I'm ambitious to work, and to do good work, but I'm the least ambitious person," she considers. "I've never known how to sell myself." At the same time, the voracious range of projects is partly due to her refusal to admit self-doubt. "I've never said, 'Can I do this?'" she admits. "I've just leapt in. If I'd ever stopped to think I'd never have done it."

"All my influences helped when it came to do *Cats*," she considers. "There was no story, so it was totally carried by the dance." Lloyd Webber's theatrical adaptation of poems by TS Eliot was an improbable hit; Michael Billington, reviewing the 1981 premiere for the *Guardian*, praised "an exhilarating piece of total theatre" that, he declared, demolished the myth that British dancers lagged behind America. Noting that "the show is packed with dance but it never kills the language or overpowers the strong individual

characterisation," he praised the Jellicle Ball, which "with its somersaults, spins and catapult-motion, has that quality of terpsichorean joy I last saw in Bob Fosse's *Dancin'*."

Although the gymnastic aspect of *Cats* drew attention, Lynne maintains that its style is indebted to her early training. "Everything I've done," she told me in 2005, "even laced all the way through *Cats*, has a strong classical basis." Classical training will always catch her eye in auditions – when casting *Chitty Chitty Bang Bang*, she said, "I threw out a lot of people who were quite delicious to look at, but there was nothing classical in there. If you haven't had that technique, it won't have the line. I look for it all the time."

Lynne's story of the visit to the doctor that sent her to dance classes inspired the book *Epiphany* by educationalist Sir Ken Robinson, and he cites it when arguing that schools too often ignore creative intelligence. "We have to rethink the fundamental principles on which we're educating our children," he claims. Lynne herself is chary of the academic studies that dancers are now encouraged to pursue alongside their training, even though she told a previous interviewer that "I had very poor schooling because of the war and the only thing I was any good at was divinity." "I can see how it's good," she tells me, "but some of the youngsters don't have the stamina we had. You did not ever want to be off – it's no good if you're not tough, if you don't couple the soul with a complete iron grit."

Commitment remains central to her creed. "Apart from talent, it's the only thing that

Opposite: Gillian Lynne at rehearsals for Cats. Photo credit Louanne Richards.

Above: Gillian Lynne
directing at the RSC.

really matters," she said in 2005, "because it's a hard world. You have to learn to live with pain, and you have to learn the gruelling guilt factor: that you can't achieve artistry and joy, or anything, without this body being an incredible working machine. And there are no short cuts – there are in other worlds, but not in this world."

"If you fall in love with dance," she told the Faculty conference, "it will sustain you through your life." Lynne received the RAD's Queen Elizabeth II Coronation Award in 2001, and is now a Vice President of the Academy. In 2005, she created male and female variations for the RAD's Fonteyn Nureyev Young Dancers Competition for Young Dancers. She embodies the benefits of dance in lifelong wellbeing (it is even the subject of *Longevity Through Exercise*, a fitness DVD released in 2014). Even now at 88, with two artificial hips and "a hideous half-metal foot", Lynne is fretful when unable to work.

In parting, I ask for the advice she'd pass on to a young artist. "Most of all, have antennae at the back of your head for everything that's going on," she replies. "And this is something I believe very strongly – you have to learn to disturb the air. It's no good just going into a room, whether to learn or to teach. Your duty is to disturb the air, to make that which was before, different."

GILLIAN LYNNE DBE

Gillian started her career in 1942 at age 16 before joining the Sadler's Wells Ballet Company where she became a soloist. Following a successful performing career at the London Palladium, on early British TV, and as Britain's foremost exponent of Jazz Dance, she went on to be a leading director and choreographer. Best-known for her work on 'Cats' and 'The Phantom of the Opera', Lynne has directed over 50 productions in the West End and on Broadway – most recently the West End premiere of Jerry Herman's 'Dear World' – as well as 11 feature films, and over 50 television productions.

Gillian has received two Olivier Awards, and in 2013 she was presented with a Lifetime Achievement Award at the Royal Opera House. Other awards include Vienna's Silver Order of Merit, Golden Rose of Montreux Award for the staging of 'The Muppet Show', a BAFTA for 'A Simple Man', a Moliere Award, The Queen Elizabeth II Coronation Award and in 2012 she was elected Vice-President of the Royal Academy of Dance. Gillian received a CBE in 1997 and in 2014 she was elevated to DBE.

2014 sees Gillian stage a new production of Sir Robert Helpmann's ballet 'Miracle in the Gorbals' for the Birmingham Royal Ballet, releasing a fitness DVD, and writing the sequel to her recent memoir 'A Dancer In Wartime', which is soon to be made into a feature film.

DAVID JAYS

David writes about theatre and dance for the Sunday Times, The Guardian and other publications, and is editor of Dance Gazette, the Royal Academy of Dance magazine.

Personal Reflections on Robert Cohan

BY KENNETH OLUMUYIWA THARP OBE

"I joke a lot about ageing now. You want to be sure when you look back that you don't have regrets. So, do the thing you love to the best of your ability."
Robert Cohan, 12 July 2013, speaking to students from London Contemporary Dance School at The Place.

In April last year (2013), I had the great pleasure of undertaking a public conversation with Robert Cohan CBE, as the opening event of a three-day RAD conference on the theme of Dance for Lifelong Wellbeing. It is always special talking to Bob, but it was a great privilege to be asked to conduct our conversation in front of an audience of delegates attending the conference. In preparing for the public event, I got to spend time with Bob, exploring territory that was both familiar and, in some aspects, uncharted. This was an added treat made possible largely by the fact that Bob had at that point only recently moved back to London after many years of being based in the South of France.

That some elements of our conversation were familiar wasn't so surprising given that I have known Bob as a teacher, choreographer, artistic director, mentor and guru since I was eighteen-years-old – nearly thirty-six years. I was honoured to dance for twelve and a half years in the company he founded, most of that time under his direction, which meant I spent many hours with him in the studio, in daily class, in rehearsal and under his watchful eye on stage. The surprise, however, was to find that our conversation on the theme of dance and lifelong wellbeing revealed new aspects of Bob's experience and knowledge that I had not heard him talk about before in quite this way. It was as if the hidden pieces of a jigsaw puzzle were falling gently into place. I feel privileged to have had the opportunity to, firstly, have dialogue with Bob at the conference and to re-visit that territory here, a year later. My personal Cohan jigsaw feels considerably enriched.

My insight into Bob's world has also grown exponentially in this past year, thanks to the publication of Paul R.W. Jackson's biography, entitled *The Last Guru: Robert Cohan's Life in Dance – From Martha Graham to London Contemporary Dance Theatre.* This includes (most unusually, but with great added insight), commentary by Bob on each chapter. I highly

recommend the book both as a tribute and as a chronological account of a life shaped by, and dedicated to, dance. It's also a candid and personal insight into one of dance's most distinguished individuals. Again, Paul's book has helped me appreciate and re-discover in a new light many of the things I have come to know about and learn from Bob, along with things I've discovered anew.

Let me start by saying that Bob is one of the most remarkable people I have ever met. He has had an enormous impact and influence on my life and work, through his teaching, directing and through his example. Indeed through simply being the person that he is, he has probably done more to change me – not just within the confines of dance – than any one other single person, notwithstanding my parents. The crucial thing to add here is that I know this thought is not unique to me, but is probably shared by just about every one of the dancers who trained daily with Bob in London Contemporary Dance Theatre (LCDT) during its 27–year existence. And I'm sure similar sentiments are likely true for many of the dancers who passed through the London Contemporary Dance School, whilst he was Artistic Director of The Place.

As someone who had only studied classical ballet from the age of five, my perceptions of dance were blown apart at the age of 16 by my first encounter with Robert Cohan's LCDT. That quickly led me to The Place, to gradually acquire not simply a whole new way of moving, but rather another way of looking at and thinking about dance and movement. That

is not to say that I regret for a second or did not find useful my early training in classical ballet, which served me well in other ways. But I acknowledge that it was from this starting point that Bob began to shape and influence my life as a dancer and beyond.

When, together with Bob, I began thinking about the notion of dance and lifelong wellbeing, we both noted that there were possibly two very different or perhaps parallel ways to approach the subject. One channel of thought was to focus on the notion of wellbeing first and then try to answer the questions: if optimum wellbeing and life enhancement were the goals, what experience of dance might one seek? How far, for example, would participation in a weekly salsa class promote individual wellbeing? Or, what are the lasting effects of watching dance regularly? Another approach was to question how could one pursue a vocation in dance, performing as a professional at the highest possible level, and at the same time maintain optimum wellbeing? How far can one make huge demands on the dancer, whilst seeking to minimise the negative impacts on body, mind and spirit? Is it possible to single-mindedly pursue the goal of perfection, and also maintain wholeness? I'm not sure how far we managed to answer those essential questions in our conversation, but it was then and now a useful springboard to touch on aspects of dance that are perhaps too rarely discussed.

In my personal journey I spent years training for, and aspiring to be, a dance artist capable of performing in a world-class

Opposite: Robert Cohan rehearsing Bob Smith of LCDT. Photo credit Anthony Crickmay.

Above: Robert Cohan – courtesy of The Place.

company. At the same time, throughout my whole performing career, I was also teaching, not only in vocational schools, youth dance companies and university settings, but often in secondary and primary schools, working with children and young people who sometimes had little or no dance experience. In fact, my first two weeks on a full-time contract with LCDT were spent in a two-week residency in a school in Hampshire. I enjoyed this aspect of my work, not only because it challenged me as a teacher to be incredibly clear, but it also taught me early on that dance was capable of transforming and enriching young lives in so

many ways. I watched young people discover the joy of dancing, self-awareness, confidence, courage, tenacity, grit, self-discipline, empathy, creative thinking and teamwork. As a result, I never doubt that dance, along with the other arts, has an absolutely central role to play as part of a rounded and holistic education. I don't believe any young person will discover and develop their full range of talents and attributes simply sitting at a desk. My lifelong passion for nurturing young talent and creative learning was sparked in LCDT.

In 2011 Bob was invited to write a short piece for an issue of *Dance UK News* in which he spoke with characteristic eloquence and precision about the benefits of dance as an education. He began by saying: "Dance education is an education for living", and ended with the simple statement: "The study of dance will give you tools with which to enhance your life." He also explained how dance teaches you a whole host of things: awareness of your body, how you exist in space, logic, relationships, how to pay attention, how to push further than one thought possible, how to express things that perhaps cannot be said, how to be comfortable in your body.

These observations chime closely with my own experience and with the thinking of other experts in the field of learning and creativity such as Sir Ken Robinson and Howard Gardiner, who subscribe to theories of multiple intelligence. Dr Anthony Seldon from Wellington College (who has just received a knighthood for Services to Education) built his school's 'Octagon' model around eight difference types of intelligence, or 'aptitudes', as he calls them, and in a recent meeting with arts professionals he shared his view that for young people "art is not just an entitlement but a psychological need", that "creativity has to be in everything, not just in a 4 to 5pm slot – creative intelligence underlies all other [types of intelligence]."

Of all the attributes that dance can bring to an individual, for me the most crucial one – which Bob and I touched on in our conversation last year – is how dance teaches one to be totally 'present', to be grounded in the here and now. Of course dance is not the only thing capable of doing that; I experienced it with equal clarity a couple of weeks ago, when I was sea-kayaking on the West Coast of Scotland. There are moments when the dynamic experience of riding the waves really feels akin to dancing. My background in dance no doubt helps with balance, but the most crucial observation I made just after having paddled for over two hours on a 10km crossing between the Isle of Muck and the mainland (in what were probably the most challenging and unpredictable conditions I had paddled in), was that the circumstance forced me to be absolutely in the present moment, with full concentration and awareness. The experience of being present is, for me, the golden thread that connects dance with what might also be experienced in meditation, or playing music, or in the act of painting, or in anything that encourages, if not requires, that state of being. This perhaps is the most important ingredient that dance can offer in terms of personal

development and wellbeing. And, to be clear, I do not think this experience is the prerogative only of the 'professional' dancer, though they may perhaps experience it at another level.

As a dancer in Bob's company, I believe he helped develop in us the art of being present every day that we were in the studio taking class or rehearsing, as well as when we were on stage. I remember Christopher Bannerman, who also danced with LCDT, sharing the reflection that "Bob just didn't teach us how to *dance*, he taught us how to *be*". I think Chris was absolutely right. When people talk about someone having 'stage presence', they also sometimes talk about 'charisma', or the suggestion that someone possesses some unquantifiable 'X-factor', but I am certain that the most compelling performers and performances rely on way more than a charismatic personality. The magic happens when an individual or company of dancers find that clear state of being totally focused in the present, eschewing anxieties about what just happened or is about to happen.

"Is dancing good for you?" I asked Bob. His answer was unsurprisingly not as simple as a yes or no. I'm sure we were both aware that the intense and extremely diverse range of demands faced by a dancer requires them to be extraordinarily focused, resilient, adaptable, strong and flexible. It requires huge mental and physical stamina and the dancer is often every bit the athlete. At the same time dancers need to be highly attuned to whole range of aesthetic demands, in the studio and on stage, in the creation of a piece and in its performance, whilst

Above: Robert Cohan –
courtesy of The Place.

balancing this with a technical perfection.
We require that dancers are hugely empathetic,
creative and unafraid to take on new challenges,
to be a strong team-player and yet at the same
time to have single-minded determination,
self-confidence and self-awareness.

Nowadays, in a highly competitive industry,
dancers inevitably vie for jobs and roles,
choreographers are often expected to break
boundaries and conquer new frontiers by
challenging their dancers to their limits, and
schools training dancers have the almost
impossible task of preparing them for an
extraordinarily diverse sector. How then do
we help protect the dancer from allowing the
pressure to achieve short-term goals outweigh
a lifetime of potential problems and ill-health?
And what can we do to help them meet the
demands of the job *and* maintain optimum health,

avoiding a catalogue of potential pitfalls such
as chronic injury, eating disorders and more?

What is special about dance is that it
demands the *whole* person. This is dance's gift
and, at its best, dance can lead to transformation
and to wholeness. I know that this has been
central to Bob's outlook. Take for example, the
young boy who suffers from Attention Deficit
Disorder, who finds it hard in the studio to keep
his concentration for more than a couple of
minutes at a time without becoming distracted.
When he gets on stage, however, he is totally
present and finds absolute focus. For me, this
is dance at its best. Dance helps the individual
attain wholeness, not as therapy, but of itself
as an art form. But if dance demands the whole
person, and encourages it, it also presumes for
those who aspire to a career on stage that even
at a young age – often by the time we enter into

full-time training and certainly by the time we move into the profession – somehow we have already attained that state of wholeness. And as we know, for some dancers, no matter how talented, that wholeness is still sometimes out of reach, or it's hard for them to keep it firmly within their grasp. I'm not seeking to blame anyone for this, least of all the dancer. It's perhaps more simply just a fact of life, and each of us can, in our own way, spend a lifetime searching for complete wholeness.

There are too many myths suggesting that to be a truly effective leader, one has to be ruthless and didactic to the extreme; that dancers need taming like wild animals by a whip-cracking circus master in order to excel. Bob's example showed me early in my career how misguided such notions are. Bob has always been passionate and energised, and knows how to get results, but he has never been a raving despot. In his quietly spoken, dignified manner he could energise a room just by his presence. By the time I joined LCDT Bob had built the ethos of the daily training to such a point that all he had to do before daily company class started, was walk in the room, turn the chair round backwards so he could sit astride and lean with his elbows on the back to watch us, and simply say the word "*And…*" We would sweat our buns off for the next 90 minutes.

With set floor work, many standing exercises set in sequence (albeit with variations that could be introduced) and an accompanist who knew the work intimately, we could go for at least 20 minutes or more without stopping, linking one exercise to the next. Not only did

this build up the stamina we needed, Bob has said he also took this approach very specifically so we didn't have to think about *what* we were doing, but could focus all our energy and attention on *how* we were doing it. We had space to listen to our bodies, to work deeper, to constantly refine our practice, and find individual autonomy within a shared ritual. In this sense company class was way, way more than just a warm up for the day's rehearsal or performance – it was the place where one felt one was carving out one's craft, honing oneself to be the best instrument possible. This may not have been about wellbeing, but it was certainly about personal growth and development.

Another of Bob's many skills as a teacher was his ability to use metaphor to create an image that would stick, that would create intention. He revealed the essence of what we were trying to achieve with each exercise and movement: how to direct one's energy, where to place your attention. Perhaps most notably, his ability to transmit the kinaesthetic understanding of what a movement should *feel* like (as opposed to *look* like) was highly developed, and I often think that this one thing was hugely instrumental in allowing him to nurture such great dancers. "More" was an often used word; if Bob thought you could do more, he'd push for it. But he also sparked the desire in each of his dancers to be the best that they could be.

And if all that sounds too serious for comfort, it's hard to underestimate the power and influence of a gifted teacher who also has a well-developed sense of humour. One day in

the studio, after demonstrating an exercise to us, he caught me starting to over-analyse, and when I began to say, "Yes, but I feel…" he swiftly interjected and said, "I don't care how YOU feel, it's how *I* feel." A good laugh stopped me in my tracks and taught me that this was a moment to learn by doing rather than getting stuck in my head. That said, I've often thought that the kind of dancers Bob looked for, beyond having the necessary physical attributes and skills, were people who were hungry, curious, hardworking; dancers who he believed would not allow themselves to remain merely as automatons. Bob sought people who were ready to become autonomous, self-determining individuals, and who could also be effective and generous team players. It was perhaps no coincidence that LCDT, which had none of the formal hierarchy of a traditional ballet company was often described as a 'company of soloists'.

Reading Paul Jackson's biography of Bob was a great reminder of what an incredible range and depth of intellect and personal insight Bob brought to each moment with his dancers. His interests and knowledge encompassed everything from Zen Buddhism, philosophers such as Gurdjieff and Krishnamurti, ornithology, bio-mechanics, classical music and much more. A teacher can lead you to question by sparking your curiosity, but a great teacher doesn't just answer your question, instead leading you toward self-

Opposite: Kenneth Tharp and Robert Cohan – courtesy of The Place.

Above: Kenneth Tharp and Robert Cohan at the RAD conference.

discovery. Knowledge and self-awareness are perhaps best valued when you feel you have discovered them for yourself, but hindsight and reflection will also incite realisation that you might not have had those discoveries without the right teacher to point you in the right direction. That's how I feel about Bob. He has spent his life pointing many people in the right direction.

Last July, following a terrific week of graduation performances at The Place by London Contemporary Dance School students, the entire School's staff and students, along with families and friends, gathered in the theatre for the end of term leavers' ceremony. Without doubt one of the special highlights of this inevitably poignant and yet celebratory occasion was the address that Bob Cohan gave to the students. Below, from the notes I took, are some highlights, to give you a taste of and insight into a man who, at almost ninety, imparts wisdom based on a lifetime of experience, with such clarity and insight:

> "Perhaps a lot of other people are giving you advice. My advice to you is to take their advice."

> "I often think how lucky we are to be in dance … if you love your job you'll never do another day of work in your life." (via Confucius)

> "When I decided to become a dancer my father said: 'Get out of this house!'… which I did. I never looked back."

> "I didn't have to make the choice to dance. The choice was made for me."

> "Martha Graham said: 'the body never lies'. As a dancer you go on the stage and there's no way you can lie."

> "Most importantly, everybody wants to do better. There are ways of getting there that allow you to remain honest to yourself."

> "As a dancer there's no excuse for not always doing your very best. Your job as a dancer is to enlighten the audience."

> "So my advice is to be honest and open (easy to say, hard to do), but that's the job. Take class every day, and work hard."

> "Dance is not hard if you approach it as the real thing. It's hard if you're not sure."

> "Cultures are remembered for their artists and their warriors, not for their business efficiency. You are the special group – the artists."

> "I joke a lot about ageing now. You want to be sure when you look back that you don't have regrets. So, do the thing you love to the best of your ability."

These to me were priceless words, and it was clear from the enormously enthusiastic response, how well Bob's comments had been able to connect with the students in particular, as well as with the rest of the audience. But I am not surprised at this; Bob has always demonstrated a canny ability to get to the heart of the matter and communicate in a way that leaves a lasting impression. I am enormously grateful for everything that Bob has taught me – and is still teaching me – on my own path to lifelong learning and wellbeing.

Reference

Dance UK News. 80. Spring (2011). Print.

ROBERT COHAN CBE

Robert Cohan trained at the Martha Graham School, and began his career in the Martha Graham Dance Company in 1946. As soloist, he performed as a partner to Graham herself before starting his own dance group in 1957 and starting a career as a choreographer.

In 1967, he became the first Artistic Director of the Contemporary Dance Trust in London and the founder Artistic Director of The Place, London Contemporary Dance School and London Contemporary Dance Theatre. In this time, Robert was instrumental in growing a vast following, not only for the work of LCDT but through his pioneering residencies which laid the groundwork for the many other British companies that followed.

As director of LCDT he created many works in collaboration with leading composers and designers such as Stages, No Man's Land, Stabat Mater, Forest and Testament. Many of his works have also been shown by the BBC.

Since 1989 he has choreographed for the Scottish Ballet as well as companies in Germany, Italy and Israel. In the US, Robert has taught at The Julliard School, Harvard, Radcliffe, and the University of Rochester, as well as York University in Toronto and many UK institutions.

With LCDT he won the 1975 Evening Standard Award for The Most Outstanding Achievement in Ballet and in 1978 a similar award from the Society of West End Theatre. He also holds honorary doctorates from the Universities of Kent, Exeter, Middlesex and Winchester. In 1988 Robert was awarded an honorary CBE for his outstanding contribution to dance in UK. He has since taken British nationality.

In 2005, Robert's 80th birthday was celebrated with a symposium at The Place and a gala performance at Sadler's Wells in London. In 2013, he was awarded the De Valois Award for Outstanding Achievement at the 2012 Critics' Circle National Dance Awards.

KENNETH OLUMUYIWA THARP OBE

Kenneth Tharp is Chief Executive of The Place, the UK's premier centre for contemporary dance. Kenneth trained at the London Contemporary Dance School, and his 25-year performing career included London Contemporary Dance Theatre (1981–1994), Kim Brandstrup's Arc Dance Company (1994–2005) and the Nigel Charnock Company. He has also worked extensively as a choreographer, director and teacher, including at The Royal Ballet School and Millennium Performing Arts and was co-director of Artyfartyarts, a multidisciplinary arts group. He served on the Board of the Royal Opera House from 2002–2010 and was Visiting Professor at the University of Lincoln from 2009–2012. In 2013 he joined the Cultural Learning Alliance Steering Group. He has been named in five successive Powerlists of Britain's 100 most influential black people (2010–2014), and appears in Who's Who. In 2003 he was made an OBE in recognition of his services to dance.

In Conversation: Lauren Cuthbertson and Anne Hogan

ANNE: How has being a dancer impacted your perspective on health and wellbeing? A career in ballet certainly poses physical and emotional challenges – are there benefits as well for dancers' overall health?

…

LAUREN: The endorphins and adrenaline you get from doing something you love every day are incredible. I have fun every day, even when there are stresses I can always manage to laugh at myself. Life in a company gives you a sense of collective purpose – whether in class or performing, there is a wonderful sense of camaraderie among hard-working professionals, all of whom are passionate about what they do. Dancing professionally also gives you a sense of achievement that replenishes the strains that go with it. You lay everything out there – dancing allows you to express an intense emotional range, so you feel like you're living life to the full, which is what we crave in life.

…

ANNE: Is it difficult to cope with the emotional intensity of the roles you perform?

…

LAUREN: I do struggle with the excess adrenaline after a performance. You can't ignore the emotional pressure, even with a role like Aurora (which I performed last night), that doesn't have as many layers as Manon, for instance, or Juliet. To stay balanced, you have to go softly with yourself, to chill out and to pace yourself, though admittedly, sometimes schedules don't allow much time for that.

But the importance of physical and emotional recovery is crucial; I've had to develop means of making space for that through my career. Dancers need to take a free weekend once in a while – the body needs it. If I can manage a free weekend, for instance, I will take Saturday completely off and maybe do some Pilates on the Sunday.

…

ANNE: Is Pilates part of your regular training routine? How do you manage to stay sufficiently fit for the range of roles you perform without overdoing it?

…

LAUREN: I have a pool of supplementary training methods to draw on. It all depends on what I crave. I know when I'm missing something, and I adjust my training to emphasise strength or length depending on what I need at a particular time. I might swim, do Pilates or a bit of strength conditioning.

Opposite: Lauren Cuthbertson as Juliet in The Royal Ballet's *Romeo and Juliet* (Sir Kenneth MacMillan). Photo credit Bill Cooper.

I have a 20 minute warm-up of core exercises that I do before class (or by the pool on swimming days). When I was younger, I wasn't particularly in touch with my body, but I've developed the ability to listen to what it needs.

...

ANNE: You have had to struggle with illness and injury at several points in your career. How did you find the resilience to cope with time off and to regain the strength to perform?

...

LAUREN: When I look back at my injuries, and having to take 16–18 months off twice in my life, I don't know how I didn't lose the fight – I feel like the Terminator!

The first time I experienced injury was when I was 19 or 20. I had a stress fracture and it was the first real pain I'd ever felt. But the recovery was straight forward – you put on the boot, and when the bone has healed, you go back to work.

In 2008, I came down with glandular fever, and that was something else entirely. I had pushed through incredible fatigue, and when the test results finally confirmed the illness, I didn't know how I'd get better, or when, or if I even would at all. My body and brain felt like they were in a thick fog.

...

ANNE: That must have felt devastating – how did you manage to recover?

...

LAUREN: At first, I just had to rest. After six months, I was up to doing a 20 minute walk a day. I suppose I must have been depressed, but eventually I gained confidence from tiny improvements, like taking two hours, not three, to get out of bed after a siesta. I kept a diary, and now and then I read it to remember what I went through. I wrote in one passage that I couldn't imagine putting my hand on a barre again. My muscles had completely gone, they were like spaghetti. But little by little I knew I was improving, that I would get there. I started back to training with Jackie Barrett, who is my 'fairy godmother'. Our first session lasted only 5 minutes; that was all the energy I had. We went gradually to 5–10 minutes at the barre, two or three times a week. I'd been away from it so long that it felt surreal – it took 9 months to get my *developpé* back. It made me realise how strong dancers are when they're in top shape, and helps me appreciate where I am now. You have to take stock and value what's positive in your life.

...

ANNE: What was it like to perform again?

...

LAUREN: I came back in 2010, and had some of the best seasons I'd ever had, including Christopher Wheeldon creating the title role for me in *Alice's Adventures in Wonderland*. But by 2012, I had developed multiple spurs and calcium in my ankle joint, and couldn't put weight on my right foot. Luck didn't seem to be on my side – the surgeon said to me, "Never mind *Swan Lake*, I don't know if you'll walk again."

...

ANNE: Awful! Were people supportive of you at this time?

...

LAUREN: The Royal Ballet couldn't have been more supportive, and while my family and friends felt like they were in shock too, they were wonderful. But I suppose that, after my second operation, some people hadn't understood quite how sensitive my ankle was; the damage that had been done to it through misdiagnosis and incorrect rehab.

…

ANNE: You're dancing your full repertoire beautifully now. Does the injury continue to impact your dancing in any way?

…

LAUREN: I've become hypersensitive to what my right foot needs. I allowed for time in between performances, for instance, to build up strength for *allegro*. Fortunately, I have coaches I trust and who support me fully, and I use rehearsals as a form of rehab. I've learned that you don't need to rehearse full-out all the time. Using visualisation and holding back on some things until you're on stage helps keep your performances fresh.

…

ANNE: What do you see as the biggest challenges, with regard to health and wellbeing, for dancers?

…

LAUREN: The fact that it's such a short career makes for big challenges. Time becomes squashed for a dancer, and because you want to do as much as you can in the time you have, there's never enough recovery time. Many dancers go for short-term fixes to injury or periods of stress. But to a certain extent, you can opt to pace yourself appropriately, to take

things one day at a time, push when you need to push, and pull back when you can. Stress and anxiety just make the muscles tight. Of course, dancers are the tools of the choreographer. I mean that in a good way; it's what we trained to do, but it means that we don't always have the option to control the demands put on us.

…

ANNE: What are some of your coping mechanisms for particularly full rehearsal or performance periods?

…

LAUREN: It's healthy to remember times when you felt in a good place physically and

Above: Lauren Cuthbertson in The Royal Ballet's *Live Fire Exercise* (Wayne McGregor) with Federico Bonelli. Photo credit Bill Cooper.

emotionally, to recall that state when things get stressful. You also have to maintain a sense of perspective – to say to yourself, "What can I work on from this in a positive way?" Ultimately, it's all towards the show – you prepare yourself to give the best performance you can at that moment. Rehearsals are fantastic to achieve and strive for better and greater technique. They are also there to work on details of the character but it's crucial to remember that you are working towards something that's for the show. Ballet is an art form and it happens when the curtain goes up, so you need to bring everything together for that moment. You're not relaying a perfect rehearsal, you're giving a live show and that's fundamentally what the most important thing is.

LAUREN CUTHBERTSON

Born in Devon, Lauren trained at The Royal Ballet School from 1995 to 2002. She won a Silver Medal at the RAD's Genée International Ballet Competition in 2001, when she also won Young British Dancer of the Year. Having joined The Royal Ballet in 2002, she was promoted to Soloist in 2003, First Soloist in 2006 and Principal in 2008. Her awards include Outstanding Female Artist at The Critics National Dance Awards (2004), the Silver Medal at the International Ballet Competition at Varna (2006), and Arts and Culture Woman of the Future in 2008.

Her repertoire includes Odette/Odile, Giselle, Aurora, Lilac Fairy, and Princess Florine, Cinderella, Juliet, Sugar Plum Fairy, Myrtha, Manon and Lescaut's Mistress, Nikiya and Gamzatti, Mitzi Caspar, 'M' (Ek's Carmen) Polyhymnia, Tombeaux, Symphony in C (second movement), Agon, Requiem, Polyphonia, DGV:Danse a grande vitesse, La Valse, Serenade, Dances at a Gathering, Voluntaries, Les Sylphides, Les Patineurs, Diamonds (Jewels), Sweet Violets.

She created La Glace (Les Saisons), Alice (Alice in Wonderland) and roles in Tryst, Qualia, Chroma, Infra, Acis and Galatea (Royal Opera), Live Fire Exercise, Carbon Life, The Human Seasons, Tetractys, The Art of Fugue and The Winter's Tale.

ANNE HOGAN

A former member of the Boston Ballet Company and Pacific Northwest Ballet, Anne holds a BA in English Literature from Harvard University, and an MA and PhD in English Literature from Brown University. She taught in the Department of English and Comparative Literature and was Director of Alumni Relations at The American University of Paris, and was previously the Head of Dance Studies at the University of Wolverhampton, and Head of Postgraduate Studies and Research at London Contemporary Dance School. Prior to joining the RAD as the Director of Education, she was an Associate Dean in the Faculty of Humanities, Arts, Languages and Education at London Metropolitan University.

Anne has taught English and Comparative Literature, specialising in Shakespeare in performance, as well as both theoretical and practical courses in Performing Arts, specialising in dance. Anne's edited publications include Balanchine Then and Now (Sylph Editions and the Arts Arena, 2008) and recent conference presentations include 'Beating the Bad Rap: Ballet and/as Somatic Practice' (University of Coventry).

Into the Wings: Steering the Transition from Performer to Teacher

BY DENNIE WILSON

Given the nature of their profession, dancers innately understand that their career is a relatively short one. Inevitably, a point of transition will be reached and a centre stage career will begin to *bourée* gently towards the wings. The reality, however, of this swan song (so to speak), does not quite correlate with the image of a feathered creature floating effortlessly across the water. For many dancers, a complex struggle to navigate their career transmutation takes place out of sight, just below the surface.

In his 2002 article on career transitions for dancers, Stanley Greben suggests that: "understanding the dancer's challenges in transition requires recognising the interplay between the external factors and those that are intrinsic to the individual dancer" (17). The balance of circumstances central to a decision to retire from performing, he argues, is counteracted by the psychological make-up of the individual dancer. The transition is particularly complex when the external factors significantly shape the decision-making process. Like a professional footballer whose career is cut short by injury, a loss of form or replacement by another player, a dancer may find themselves a victim of circumstances over which they have little control.

As programme manager for the RAD portfolio of teaching qualifications designed specifically for professional dancers, I find myself reflecting on the audition and interview process and considering what it is that drives some dancers to choose teaching as their next profession. Applicants come from across the world (many study with English as their second or third language) and from across the dance spectrum: ballet and contemporary dance companies; musical theatre and the commercial sector; and project-based work, where they balance performance with teaching, choreographing, coaching and project management. Many note the sense of responsibility they feel to pass on the knowledge acquired throughout their performing careers to the next generation of dancers. I have heard many stories of dancers agreeing to do some teaching and discovering a hidden passion for it as they witness a transformation, however small, within a student they are working with.

My work with professional dancers began as my own career evolved into that of a freelance teacher and choreographer.

Working as a dance artist with Birmingham Royal Ballet, I began mentoring company dancers who were enrolled on an affiliated BA/MA programme and who had an interest in delivering aspects of the company's outreach programme. My work with Birmingham Royal Ballet spanned 10–12 years and afforded significant texture to my professional life, as it required me to adopt an entirely different mindset to that of delivering vocational training or large scale community dance projects. In joining the RAD's Faculty of Education (FoE), I was aware of the opportunity to progress and refine my practice and contribute to the development of the FoE's provision for professional dancers.

Professional Dancers Teaching Diploma

The RAD teaching awards for professional dancers emerged at a moment in which the UK dance sector began to formally recognise the challenges dancers face at the end of their careers. 1973 saw the establishment of the Dancer's Resettlement Fund, which offered retraining support to dancers from the five companies then funded by the Arts Council, and which has since evolved into the Dancers Career Development (DCD). Representing a sea change within the professional dance sector, the DCD continues to provide dancers with career support and retraining, helping them to think about life after performance and the need for continuing professional development.

In 1974, the RAD announced the start of a four-month concentrated course to help dancers wishing to follow their stage careers by entering the teaching profession. Six students successfully completed the course, which was expanded the following year to a five-month intensive course, attracting thirteen students from six different countries. Originally known as the Professional Dancers Teaching Course (PDTC), this has become the highly popular Professional Dancers Teaching Diploma (PDTD), delivered on-site at the RAD headquarters in London from June to August.

Professional Dancers' Postgraduate Teaching Certificate

2014 sees the 40th anniversary of the PDTD. Many of its graduates have pursued careers training future dancers in vocational areas, while others have opted to explore the growing opportunities for dance teachers within the public sector. Over the same period, dancers' expectations about the time span of their performing careers has, to some extent, shifted, as advances in dance injury care and prevention have resulted in some enjoying prolonged careers. As a result, more and more dancers are looking to begin their career transition while still performing.

The RAD recognises the need to design programmes that meet the shifting needs of dancers, and that address the growth of dance provision across a range of sectors. In January 2013, it expanded its portfolio of programmes with the launch of the Professional Dancers' Postgraduate Teaching Certificate – Berlin (PDPTC).

Designed to complement the successfully

Opposite: The PDPTC 2013 cohort with Dennie (back row 2nd right).

established PDTD programme, the PDPTC has been devised to more fully accommodate the requirements of dancers with increasingly diverse performing careers and aspirations. The year-long, part-time programme, which is delivered on-site and by distance learning, offers dancers an opportunity to gain a teaching qualification whilst still working and performing. Its flexible delivery also appeals to former dancers who may already have embarked on teaching careers. Following a week-long on-site induction, modules studied by distance and teaching placements (January to June and September to November) accommodate the dancers' rehearsal, performance and work schedules. The July Summer Intensive period brings the dancers together to study, share, debate, examine, be examined and, in short, begin to feel equipped for careers as dance teachers.

The PDPTC's development has been supported by an advisory group with long-standing experience in helping dancers to not only flourish as performers, but also to constructively realign their skills towards other vocations. The group consists of Gianni Malfer, Managing Director of Danse Suisse, Professor Martin Puttke, Ballet Master and creator of the DANAMOS movement system, and Dr Christiane Theobald, Deputy Director of the Stattsballett Berlin, which has generously hosted the on-site element of the PDPTC programme in its stunning, purpose-built studios.

Christiane has observed that dancers are often reluctant to talk with their directors about their career beyond performance for fear of them being overlooked when it comes to casting. She considers it essential, however, that a dancer is able to consider their career transition whilst continuing to work, and not face a long period of unemployment as they retrain. Many directors share Christiane's efforts to encourage supportive exchange about career transitions between dancers and their artistic managers.

Two stages

Environments in which dancers feel comfortable discussing or initiating their eventual move from performing, however, remain sporadic at best. Acclaimed ballerina Lynn Seymour has spoken of how companies do not actively look to "lengthen the careers" (Newman, 61) of their dancers. She also comments that dancers:

> "…don't start teaching in the company or start taking rehearsals while they're still dancing [...] I don't know why, lack of imagination basically. If you are in the company dancing, why can't you help some of the young dancers learn something? … It is, actually a waste of resource. A misuse of a great resource … or no use." (61)

Taking into consideration his own career as well as that of other dancers who began to teach within more receptive environments, Desmond Kelly, former Artistic Director at Elmhurst School for Dance and Assistant Director of Birmingham Royal Ballet, suggests that there are two stages to the transition from performing:

Photo credit Benedict Johnson.

"At first they are the dancer who begins by teaching themselves through reflection and critical engagement with the information they receive from their teachers.

Then they adopt the active role of teaching others (whilst still dancing) and through approaching the learning of dance from a different perspective, their own dancing improves." (Newman 108).

Both Desmond's and Lynn's observations suggest that the dancer as teacher can become a great resource for a company. They also support the idea that whilst a performance career might not tap into every part of a dancers' ability, it inevitably refines their natural intelligence and versatility.

Observing career transitions

The PDTD and the PDPTC address the complex pressures that dancers face as they embark upon their teaching vocation. Their design and delivery are informed by the psychological and physical particularities of a dancers' career shift, and by the multifaceted context of dance education today, ranging as it does from technique class to repertoire, to performance coaching to dance fitness and rehabilitation.

A session on career transitions at the RAD's Dance for Lifelong Wellbeing Conference offered the opportunity to share expertise and to examine current tensions within the professional sector. The session featured an interview with Gary Avis, who has had a very distinguished career with the Royal Ballet. Gary still performs with the company as a Principal Character Dancer alongside his relatively new role as Ballet Master.

Gary observed that his work in the studio now requires him to both face and turn away from the 'mirror'. This shift in focus has brought with it a multitude of additional responsibilities and challenges, from negotiating his role as both colleague and coach to fellow company members, to fluctuating feelings of acceptance and loss for his previous role as, exclusively, a performer. Gary described his career transition as a shift of identity that entailed, at least in part, an extended period of mourning. His poignant commentary encapsulated many of the overarching issues dancers in professional flux encounter.

Maintaining the body

A dancer's body is their instrument; they become habituated to being in full command of their physique to perform extraordinary feats of technique and artistry. The moment when dancers begin to sense that their body is an ageing instrument can be a particularly complicated and sensitive time. As they get older, dancers need to do more work to prepare for the physical demands of a working day.

They tend to arrive at work much earlier, in order to spend additional time in the studio getting their bodies ready for class, rehearsal and performance.

A change in routine

When the dancer does decide to retire from performing (and it's important to consider that not all dancers are able to make this decision independently), the ritual of daily class is often the hardest habit to let go of. One's sense of identity has been bound up with the process of preparing through class for rehearsal and performance. Suddenly the purpose of something that has been done daily since a very young age evaporates, and with that, part of the personality disappears. As if these matters are not enough to cope with, the process of retraining brings with it a whole new set of challenges for the dancer to navigate.

Learning to learn again

Greben notes that it is easy to "underestimate the intelligence required to become a professional dancer" and that "as a group dancers tend to be intelligent, multi-talented and highly motivated"(15). The pursuit of a stage career, however, often results in formal education taking a back seat. The typical cycle of the trainee dancer begins between the ages of 16–19, when they embark on vocational training in which unremitting, dedicated studio time is imperative to their physical and creative progress. As the student becomes the dancer and enters a company, rehearsal, touring and performance schedules impact on any time they might have to continue or return to their formal education. Used to being directed and corrected, often required to perform in a group, dancers are disciplined, precise and respond effectively to instruction. In spite of these finely honed qualities, Greben observes that those who retrain within educational settings need considerable support and guidance, as they tend to regard themselves as "much less talented and able to learn in areas other than dancing"(15).

My experience as a programme manager and mentor supports these observations. With each new cohort of dancers, I come face to face with highly accomplished individuals who are not yet able to see their formidable set of transferable skills, skills that will help them make their passage into the next stage of their professional life. The intensity of the training and performing careers, in which they are continually being told what to do, results in difficulty with trusting their own judgement. Thus they return to formal education with a consistent, underlying need for reassurance. Many dancers readily admit that they have forgotten how they learned, and yet feel the pressure and need to instantly get things. It has not, however, been my experience that this results in individuals who are frightened to ask questions, though initially, at least, the answers they seek are generally ones where you tell them exactly what to do: they are still conditioned to do as they are told.

And yet, when I reflect again on my interviews with dancers applying to the RAD's programmes, it is humbling and

Photo credit Benedict Johnson.

inspirational to listen to the quality of their thinking and ideas as they respond to a number of challenging questions. Their observations show the breadth of their experience related to training, performance coaching, choreography, somatic techniques, and education and outreach work.

When the successful applicants arrive at the RAD, full of passion for their art form and aspiring to share their significant body of knowledge, their self-discipline, motivation and determination can nonetheless collide with self-doubt as they grapple with a significant shift of identity. Their curiosity and openness to new ideas usually prompts them to persevere,

however, and through the opportunity to study and to reflect, a newfound self-confidence emerges.

Through the support of organisations like the DCD, higher education provision specifically targeted for their needs, such as that offered by the RAD, and their own talent and determination, dancers will continue to successfully refashion their careers within and beyond the world of dance. I feel proud when I look at the qualifications of the dance staff of vocational training schools around the world, seeing the letters PDTC, PDTD, PDPTC. Often these qualifications are just the start, and graduates have gone on to study dance teaching, dance science, and somatic practices at Masters level. Others become artistic directors of schools, rehearsal and ballet masters and mistresses, while others return to their home country and establish schools where the RAD approach to the learning and teaching of dance is shared with people from all walks of life.

I shall conclude with a recurring refrain from the professional dancers I have taught: "I need to move to think." Dancers explore and prosper within a diversity of career paths, but they never really stop being dancers. A profoundly embodied perceptivity is at the core of who they are, and informs their approach to everything they engage with. In my experience, dancers are by and large courageous, empathetic, generous, intelligent and intuitive people who need to move in order to make sense of and interact with the world around them. Centre-stage careers evolve, but the dancer is never really left behind.

References

Greben, Stanley E. "Career Transition in Professional Dancers". *Journal of Dance Medicine and Science* 6.1 (2002): 14–19. Print.

Newman, Barbara. *Never Far From Dancing: Ballet artists in new roles*. Oxford & New York: Routledge, 2014. Print.

DENNIE WILSON

Dennie currently works at the Royal Academy of Dance where she is responsible for the RAD's portfolio of awards for Professional Dancers. She joined the RAD's Faculty of Education in September 2012, fresh from an exciting 6-month contract working on the Olympic and Paralympic Games, where she worked as Victory Ceremony Venue Producer. Prior to this she taught contemporary dance for 8 years at Elmhurst School for Dance, the University of Wolverhampton as Senior Lecturer in Dance and Performance, and as a dance artist with the Birmingham Royal Ballet's Department of Learning.

Dennie's career as a dancer, performer and performance maker has taken her all over the world. She has created performances from three-act dance operas, to opening ceremonies for venues ranging from the Royal Albert Hall and the National Indoor Arena Birmingham, to intimate studio spaces and art galleries. Dennie also runs a small project-based company dna3d dance design digital.

Opposite: PDPTC students with Anne Hogan (far right).

In Conversation: Robert Parker and Anne Hogan

ANNE: I'm interested in hearing about your transition from a performance career, which was, I am aware, something of a 'phased' process. When did you first begin to think seriously about life beyond performing?

…

ROBERT: I can tell you the time exactly. I was 27 and had surgery for the second time on my left knee – the reality of career mortality really hit me. I had a lot of time to reflect during the rehab period. Keeping motivated was a real challenge, and my recovery was very much 'two steps forward, one step back'. I love performing, but it was time to I ask myself, "What else would I like to do?" Then, I started to do some research.

I went to a property development seminar, and decided that wasn't for me. I was into motorcycles at the time, and considered becoming a motorcycle instructor. Then I spoke with another dancer who had got her pilot's license, and that really sparked my interest. I have always been a bit of an adrenaline junkie, so I guess I was looking for something to fill that hole left by not performing – something to give me the same sense of elation.

…

ANNE: Did you enrol on a course?

…

ROBERT: Yes, at Wellesbourne Airport in Stratford. It was so exhilarating to learn a new skill – the dancers in the company were probably sick of my telling them how many kinds of fog there are!

…

ANNE: But you eventually returned to dance. Why? What was it like to return?

…

ROBERT: I felt fortunate for having a second chance with my profession. I found I loved dancing even more – it felt like it had when I was seven. At the same time, I realised that performing wasn't everything. I thought, "Ok, I'm back, but it's inevitable that I will hit this barrier again," and I wanted to be ready. There was no longer any fear – I'd proved to myself that I could flourish outside the ballet bubble. I decided to use the rest of the time I had as a performer as wisely as possible. Especially as a principal dancer, you have a lot of downtime between performances.

…

ANNE: What did you decide to do?

…

ROBERT: I had noticed that a lot of adverts for pilot jobs said 'degree preferred', and I realised how important it was to have a qualification. At

Opposite: Robert Parker in *Apollo* (George Balanchine). Photo credit Eric Richmond.

the time, Birmingham University had an access programme for the dancers of Birmingham Royal Ballet, and I enrolled on a two-year, part-time MPhil. I also started to do some volunteer teaching at Elmhurst. I was still flying, along with doing the degree – it was a good opportunity to learn to juggle a lot of hats!

. . .

ANNE: What made you decide, for a second time, to retire from performing?

. . .

ROBERT: This amazing opportunity came up to direct Elmhurst School for Dance. I knew it would be an enriching experience, one that would equip me with new skills, and I was beginning to wind down from performing, in any case. The first time I stopped, I had no intention of returning – though I eventually did. But the second time, I knew it was really out of my system. That said, I did have a couple of last swan songs! My final performance was for the Teachers' Benevolent Fund at the Lindbury Theatre (Royal Opera House).

. . .

ANNE: You also completed the Professional Dancers' Teaching Diploma at the RAD the summer before you took over as Artistic Director of Elmhurst, so you didn't have much of a breather from your performing career! What have you found to be the biggest challenges of your new role?

. . .

ROBERT: I would say that the biggest challenge has been time management – my 'to do' list is generally about 30 miles long! I start at 7:45 and often work 11–and-a-half-hour days now, but it's not simply a question of hours. A dancer's life is largely nocturnal, so the role at Elmhurst has entailed quite a change of routine. Assuming responsibility for making decisions that will affect the lives of the students in my care has been a challenge as well; I find that you just have to trust your instinct. The need to multi-task has also been crucial to develop. It can be hard to compartmentalise, and you can feel pulled in many directions.

But when I have the chance to sit back and reflect, I can see that there have been many accomplishments. When I get a nice letter from a student or a parent, for instance, I realise that the training and the support we offer really can make a difference to the lives of young dancers. It's gratifying to see parents embrace our ethos of approachable leadership – they can see that we're not just interested in churning out great dancers, but that we have the whole person at heart. We do this in part through our links with other organisations and individuals with specialist expertise – Dance UK, the RAD, the National Institute of Dance Medicine Science (NIDMS), Birmingham University, and others.

. . .

ANNE: You spoke at the Dance for Lifelong Wellbeing conference panel discussion about the obligation to prepare students for the rigors of performance today.[1] What are some of the training initiatives you have introduced at Elmhurst?

. . .

[1] See 'Enriching Young Lives: Dance and Personal Development' panel discussion, pages 28–36.

Photo credit Richard Battye.

ROBERT: I'm particularly pleased with how well our 'Enrichment Friday' has been received. We have arranged the students' schedule so that they come off the regular timetable at 2:30 every Friday, which gives us the chance to fit in a range of events and training approaches we could not otherwise accommodate.

We use this time for activities that enhance the student experience, from Dalcroze eurhythmics, to yoga, gymnastics, swimming and other cardiovascular activities. It allows the students to let their hair down and have fun, while learning to relate other activities to their dance training.

...

ANNE: In what ways do these various activities support your students' vocational aspirations?

...

ROBERT: There are so many benefits. I found the Dalcroze system incredibly constructive with regard to my own training – it develops group skills, peripheral vision, musicality, creativity – so many necessary tools for a dancer. The aerobic/cardiovascular benefits of swimming and other activities are also crucial. As far as aerobic fitness goes, there's nothing quite like full-out rehearsing of a strenuous piece to keep you in shape, but the supplementary training does help.

…

ANNE: Has your experience as a professional dancer impacted your managerial style or leadership approach to vocational training?

…

ROBERT: It has. I am very pragmatic about student behaviour and conduct because I have a first-hand understanding of what will be expected of them in the dance world. I never patronise or condescend to students, but I do give them a reality check. I try my best to give them a clear rationale for my expectations, and they know that I am still close to the profession. I think that gives me credibility with the students – they think, "He knows what he's talking about."

…

ANNE: Do you see the demands on professional dancers increasing? If so, in which ways?

…

ROBERT: The psychological aspects of the profession are increasingly important to be aware of. Jobs are scarce, and young dancers need to be prepared to deal with the rigours of rejection. You need to support them to have realistic goals and aspirations, without taking away their dreams. To make it in the current professional climate, dancers need to go above and beyond merely sufficient – it's getting tougher out there. We stress the importance of versatility – dancers need to think outside of the box, incorporate many different dance styles and know how to collaborate with choreographers. You have to be open to diversity, to be willing to venture beyond your comfort zone. We had Adam Cooper speak with the students, for instance, and it was great because he is an example of a successful dancer who has embraced classical ballet as well as musical theatre and so many different genres.

It's not about being negative; it is about being practical and focused. I often use myself as an example, as I was told early in my training that I would never make it as a classical dancer. Students respond well to real life examples of how people overcome adversity and realise their dreams.

ROBERT PARKER

Born in Hull, Robert trained at the Royal Ballet School and joined the Birmingham Royal Ballet under the directorship of Sir Peter Wright in 1994. He became a Principal dancer in 1999 where he collaborated with newly appointed Artistic Director and acclaimed choreographer David Bintley to create many leading roles for the company.

Robert has danced a wide and varied repertoire from the classics to contemporary pieces, working with many choreographers from around the world. He has made guest appearances with the Royal Ballet and received a Critics Circle Dance Award and an Olivier Award nomination.

In 2008 he took a sabbatical from dance to acquire his Commercial Airline Pilot's License and on returning, obtained a Masters of Philosophy with the University of Birmingham. In September 2012 he became the Artistic Director of Elmhurst School for Dance in Birmingham and President of the London Ballet Association. He is also a trustee of the Dalcroze society.

RAD Outreach: Young People on the Move

BY AIDEN TRUSS

The Royal Academy of Dance is fast approaching its 100th birthday. Over the decades it has cemented its reputation as the standard bearer for ballet both in the UK and around the world. In recent years though, it hasn't so much shifted its focus as it has expanded its approach to promoting dance in all its forms, styles and genres. As a result, today it shows many different faces, reflecting its diverse membership, and it dances to many different rhythms.

On any given day, the Battersea headquarters sees the steady ebb and flow of a tide of students of all ages arriving and departing their classes. These days, however, you're as likely to feel the walls vibrating with urban dance beats and hip-hop as you are to catch the strains of the more usual suspects, like Prokofiev or Tchaikovsky.

But notions of community and inclusivity are not just buzzwords or concepts that tick the boxes of some by-the-numbers policy aimed at corporate social responsibility; they are now fundamental to the RAD's work. They underline its mission statement commitment to "removing barriers to participation in dance and to equal opportunities for all, regardless of circumstance or ability."

These are all fine intentions from an organisation with such pedigree and prestige, but what do they translate to in the 'real world' once they've left the rarefied atmosphere of the boardroom?

Alongside its work on Dance for Lifelong Wellbeing – promoting and enabling access to dance at all ages – three of the RAD's current projects centre on outreach: Step into Dance, which provides weekly after-school dance lessons to secondary school students, RADiate sessions with children with learning disabilities, and Boys Only!, which enables boys and young men to dance and benefit from positive role models. While there are obvious sensitivities around such work with the vulnerable and disadvantaged, we can paint in broad strokes a compelling picture of the highly-valued and impactful nature of these projects.

Step into Dance

Step into Dance is a partnership project between the RAD and the Jack Petchey Foundation, whose aim is to help young people "achieve their potential by inspiring, investing in, developing and promoting activities that

increase their personal, social, emotional and physical development." It is already the biggest secondary school dance programme in the UK, providing extra-curricular dance classes to over 6,000 young people in 200 schools (including Special Educational Needs/ SEN and Pupil Referral Units) across London and Essex. It also provides training courses for teachers.

Students get the opportunity to take part in a variety of performances, such as Watch this Step, Step in2 Battle, and regular Borough Events. These culminate in a showcase end-of-year experience: Step LIVE!. This has seen students perform on some of the best-known stages in London, such as the O2 Arena, Queen Elizabeth Hall, Sadler's Wells Theatre and the Southbank Centre. These prestigious venues have thus become an unlikely backdrop for the talents of youngsters from some of the most disadvantaged backgrounds in the region.

As well as taking part in classes, there are also three dance companies for which students with the best potential can audition: Street Dance, Contemporary, and Musical Theatre. Being a part of these companies provides another twenty or so performance opportunities each year.

Although Step into Dance has grown and seen hugely positive results in all the areas in which it works, it has perhaps had its most dramatic effect on the lives of young boys. This 'troubled' demographic consists of what Step into Dance Programme and Artistic Director, Sue Goodman, affectionately calls the 'Bad Boys'.

These are the young men who have seemingly little going for them socially and academically, who are seen as a problem, but who love to express themselves through dance. Through the programme they have been able to form dance 'crews' which have in some cases become surrogate families – somewhere to share experience and to forge strong bonds of friendship and encouragement. These are typically the sort of young people that might well slip through the net and end up in street gangs, but who now have a legitimate outlet for their energy and aggression, where street battles (Step in2 Battle events) are terpsichorean rather than terrifying, involving as they do breaking dance moves rather than breaking windows. This is not to make light of the situation in which many young people find themselves: for some this is a very real dichotomy, a very real choice.

And there have been other benefits too, with the schools taking part in the programme reporting measurable improvements in the schoolwork and resulting grades of the students. It seems that the outlet which dance provides is accompanied by a greater sense of aspiration. It's not clear yet as to whether this is partly due to the carrot and the stick motivation strategies of the schools, i.e. 'No homework, no dancing!' or whether the exertion just brings its own balance, catharsis and perspective to the students.

One reason cited for its success is the comparative longevity of the Step into Dance classes. Where other dance programmes might only be available for six weeks before having

Opposite: Boys Only! performance. Photo credit Roy Campbell Moore.

Above: RADiate.
Photo credit Monique Ogier.

to move on to other schools, Step into Dance has been able to maintain a stable relationship, in some instances, for years. Friern Barnet and Wanstead High School are examples of this, where Step has become an established part of the life of both the schools and with pupils regularly taking part in Borough Events. Friern Barnet School even has the programme embedded within its own 'Talented and Gifted Policy' as part of its raft of extra-curricular activities, aimed at encouraging students to maximise their potential.

Step into Dance also works in SEN schools to impart its energetic message of dance and inclusivity. One of the ways in which it does this is through the 'Step Together' initiative, in which special and mainstream schools are brought together to dance. And these sessions have had some quite unexpected results, mixing groups of very uninhibited children with special needs with their usually more reserved and self-conscious counterparts.

Much of this comes down to the fact that the SEN students possess a joie de vivre and lack of restraint that the teenagers they are paired with just don't have. They don't feel peer pressure or the need to be 'cool'. They just throw themselves into their exercises with such joyful abandon that the mainstream teenagers have found themselves really having to up their game. Where it might be thought that they would be the ones providing support to the SEN students, a real reciprocal relationship has blossomed: the less physically coordinated get help with learning steps, balance and timing, and those better able, benefit from the exuberance and confidence instilled by their opposites. It's often been a case of, "If they can do it, we can do it!", but this has developed into a truly shared experience, where both groups perform for each other and are mutually supportive. These have become important relationships for both sets of schools.

RADiate

RADiate was established in 1990 to provide subsidised dance and movement classes to children with Autistic Spectrum Disorder (ASD), as well as those with moderate to severe learning difficulties. Currently being delivered to schools in Wandsworth in South West London, the programme uses exercises carefully structured around dance in order to reach these children, many of whom normally find it a great struggle take part in group activities. Sessions are delivered by specialist tutors in collaboration with the staff at each school.

For many of these children, learning long dance sequences would be too complex an undertaking. Things need to be kept simple and so they are shown very basic dance moves, such as turns, jumps, and how to maintain their balance. And often, sensory props such as attractive multi-coloured scarves, and in some sessions, simple props such as hula-hoops are used to encourage children with autism and more complex needs to participate.

Critically, the classes are carefully structured in a way that the children can understand and follow. For those with ASD, being able to follow a pre-planned sequence of activities is an essential means of providing reassurance. All sessions begin with a 'hello song' (and end with a 'goodbye song') and follow a simple 'now and next' chain of activities to reduce the anxiety that can be a part of the condition.

Music also plays an important part in these sessions, not only to provide the rhythm for dancing, but also to help set the pace and the atmosphere of classes: warming-up, cooling down and relaxing the children.

RADiate tutor Emma Jones explained the fundamental elements of her classes where, through creative dance sessions, children are introduced to simple choreographic tasks and the basic principles of contemporary dance:

> "By creative dance sessions I mean that I use a theme or idea and we explore this creatively. Instead of pretending to be a certain animal we would instead explore the animal by thinking about how it moves (Does it jump, turn or roll? How can we jump, turn or roll in different ways?), its size (including whether or not it grows), shape (tall, wide, twisted, curved, long body shapes), its speed and if it travels using a direct or indirect pathway."

Choreographic tasks may be as simple as two children working together to create still body shapes, or as complicated as children selecting movement to create their own phrase, alone or in groups (though this will often need adult support to help in selecting movements and helping the group communicate to each other).

Basic principles of contemporary dance would be introduced through teaching simple movement phrases and discussing technical points including alignment, body control and awareness of how to be more efficient with their movements.

Due to the many difficulties these children have with communication and interaction, Makaton sign language is used in all sessions to allow everyone to communicate on a general level. As a result, these classes both accommodate and augment the children's often visual and frequently non-verbal learning style, providing alternative means for them to develop social skills and self-expression. Feedback also suggests that children reap benefits in terms of their language development, listening skills, and overall self-esteem, as well as motor skills.

One of the biggest success stories has been that of Beatrix Potter Primary School, which opened its doors to other primary schools in the area in order to share RADiate sessions and to get unfamiliar children dancing together. Led by the Borough of Wandsworth's Moderate Learning Disabilities team, along with the staff at the school, they began holding two-hour sessions, with the first

hour for children from other schools and the second with their own SEN students. The two groups of children from years 2–6, had a range of learning and physical disabilities, but the children's progress became apparent almost immediately. In their newfound friendship groups they found unexpected ways of working together that surprised even their tutors. As Sue Burton, Lead RADiate Tutor observed:

"The teacher has put together lessons that make it simple for each child to adapt movement ideas in their own way. I was impressed to see them working so hard to find their own version of a task – different to their peers – without any prompting from her or the teaching assistant."

In addition, after classes, the children are given an area in which to socialise and to take part in other artistic activities to further strengthen the new bonds they have made. Such has been the success of the scheme that the local authority in Wandsworth is now looking at rolling it out to other schools in the area.

Looking forward, the RAD is seeking funding for further development of the project. This will include taking RADiate into other boroughs, new research into the specific requirements of individual schools, documentation of research with academic partners, and the possibility of movement and dance in INSET (in-service training) sessions for school teachers.

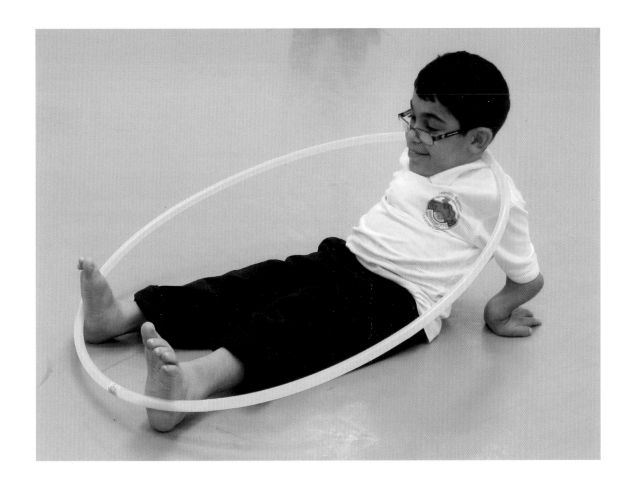

Boys Only!

Boys Only! classes are aimed at young men between the ages of 8–18 years-old, who are perennially framed in the 'hard to reach' category of problematic youth. The project began in 2005 when the RAD raised £50,000 at a *Billy Elliot: The Musical* gala evening. It put the money to work on a programme aimed at "widening participation in dance through open access events, targeted at young men with little or no dance experience." It is now a national programme with a number of regional partners around the UK who deliver ballet with a fresh perspective alongside other dance styles.

So what does this mean in plain English and how does it differ from a programme like Step into Dance?

It's all about getting young men – who already have an interest in dance – to try their hands at ballet in particular, and then to provide signposts to further opportunities for development. Ballet is the core class but

Above: RADiate.
Photo credit Monique Ogier.

Above: Step into Dance. Photo credit Foteini Christofilopoulou.

the initiative also comes with a taster of other genres (Contemporary, Bollywood, Capoeira, Street Dance) tacked on for good measure. To get past barriers in perception of the effete nature of ballet, classes aim to offer a more appealing, athletic and energetic means of teaching the art form. Alongside this is the equally important aim of providing positive male role models in an open and fun environment, especially in places where there is a lamentable paucity of both.

Like the RAD's other outreach programmes, Boys Only! had an audience just waiting to be found – boys who had had to hide their dancing passion away from others for fear of ridicule or the questioning of their masculinity. One parent even went so far as to blog about the effect that just one session had on her 'Little Man':

"When I went to pick him up seven hours later I was early […] The boys all walked out together, dressed in joggers, leotards, t-shirts, hoodies and chatting easily amongst themselves, and for the first time in a long time I saw my Little Man looking confident and at home. He was amongst his people."

Stories like this are common in the feedback from parents, teachers and carers who are constantly reporting on their amazement at how those in their care have made huge strides in improving their confidence and their behaviour. In the absence of more rigorous qualitative research into the effects of the programme to date, we have to rely upon the gushing and effusive praise from evaluation forms. But these paint a pretty clear picture of what it has achieved so far:

"I am sure that Ned will never make a dancer (!) but his interest is stimulated and he clearly enjoys it and it is wonderful that he has these opportunities."

"One of the Boys was going to give up Ballet and by taking part in Boys Only! has now decided to carry on with his training."

"I really feel that this weekend has taught Curtis that it is ok for boys to dance and to ignore nasty comments from others!"

At an age where peer pressure and opinion weigh upon young people with a crushing enormity, these seemingly small victories take on a great significance and value. Suddenly it *is* OK to dance despite what they may hear day to day from those who are cynically all too ready to knock their dreams and ridicule their ambitions.

To further its investment in the future of Boys Only!, the Frank Freeman Scholarship was set up in 2012 in memory of a popular former RAD Examiner and teacher. The funding from this allows a Boys Only! attendee each year to be awarded a free place on one of the many RAD Summer Schools. It is given to the boy who the teachers feel has made good progress and has demonstrated teamwork and focus over the two days of the course. These scholarships provide yet another way for these boys to reach up and help themselves out of their situations, to aspire to something more than their environment will usually allow them.

Looking forward

Step into Dance, RADiate and Boys Only! offer between them a small glimpse at a growing range of outreach programmes and projects being run by the RAD, but its community roots and ambitions are spreading. Where for so long access to dance with such a prestigious organisation would have been the preserve of the well-heeled (and their children), and there might only have been only one form of dance on the menu, things have changed. And, the future of the art in its many forms encompasses more than Solo Seal awards,

Genée medals and a future in the lofty and long-established traditional dance companies.

For an increasingly diverse audience, the RAD is opening its doors, both to allow people in to share what it has to offer, and for the RAD to pass through in order to venture into wider communities.

Although these are all admirable goals for the organisation, for many, dance means so much more. It is quite simply a means of redemption and a first taste of real ambition and achievement. For some it is a way to find themselves and their natural place in the world – along with those who view it in the same high-spirited fashion. And then, for others still, it is simply a way to be included, to dance with other children and to connect. It is about throwing their arms about with gleeful abandon and having the chance to simply be a child among other children, to connect on a level that needs no words; just the innocent and instinctive poetry of movement.

Acknowledgements

Many thanks to Sue Goodman, Sue Burton, Emma Jones, Monique Ogier and Sue Collins for their contributions to this piece.

AIDEN TRUSS
Aiden has a background in new media and marketing, writing journal articles and content for a wide range of organisations, most recently in the field of public health. He has had work published in text books by Oxford University Press and Jones & Bartlett. In 2013 his first novel, Gape, was published.

Aiden holds an MA in Cultural and Critical Studies and a BA in Humanities and Media. He currently works as a copywriter at the Royal Academy of Dance.

In Conversation: Step into Dance Company member Ayten Goksan and Sue Goodman

Step into Dance is a study in contrasts, offering many different genres of dance to many different types of schools and many different types of students. Its dancers originate from all over the world, and truly reflect the multiculturalism that is part of the fabric of London. It is this diversity and range of ability that makes the programme exciting and its dancers interesting.

In order to harness this range and diversity, Sue Goodman (Artistic and Programme Director) has set up three dance companies for which Step into Dance students, like Ayten Goksan, have to audition. The genres covered are street dance, contemporary dance and musical theatre.

...

SUE: Tell me a little bit about your family and background.

...

AYTEN: My Dad, Artun, was born in Lurucina in Cyprus. He speaks Turkish and Greek. He came to London at 18 to study maths and physics A-levels so that he could go to university. However, when the university fees went up my father could no longer afford to study here, so he went back to Cyprus and stayed there for a while. And then, when he was 24, he went to Hacettepe University in Turkey, which is where he met my mum. She was 18. Dad studied maths and Mum studied Turkish language and literature. Dad was involved in a lot of youth activities and was head of the student union. He was also a dancer and used to teach Cypriot folk dancing. My mum was one of his pupils. They both graduated in 1989, the same year that they got married. Dad came to London in 1990 to earn some extra money before going back to Cyprus. This plan did not materialise, which is why we are all here in London to this day!

At first, Dad was a maths tutor and then became a journalist and wrote for the *Turkish Gazette*. Now he is a driving instructor. Mum currently teaches Turkish A-levels in colleges and in Turkish school. I have two brothers and one sister. My sister is at Oxford University and studies natural sciences, and my brothers are still at school.

...

SUE: How is your Turkish, Ayten?

...

AYTEN: I can speak it fluently and also study it at school.

...

SUE: What started you dancing?

...

Opposite: Step into Dance Contemporary Youth Company. Photo credit Mark Lees.

AYTEN: When I was younger my parents used to take us all to the theatre. I remember going to see Shakespeare in the park. We also all love music and play different instruments. I think this has helped my dancing a lot. When I was three I decided that I wanted to become a ballerina, and starting nagging my mum. When I was 4 years old, I went to Sue Paddock's school of dancing in Tottenham, where we did tap, RAD ballet and jazz. I loved it! Then we were introduced to street dance at my Step into Dance class at my school, Winchmore. It felt very strange at first – like a new language – but then I really started to enjoy it.

. . .

SUE: What is it that you enjoy about street dance?

. . .

AYTEN: It is such fun, more relaxed and freer than ballet. Ballet is very strict and precise, whereas with street, your personality plays an important part – you add your own 'flavour'.

. . .

SUE: Does ballet help?

. . .

AYTEN: Ballet helps a lot with contemporary dance because I know how to point my feet! It also helps with alignment and placement.

. . .

SUE: When you auditioned for the Step into Dance Contemporary and Street Dance companies, what did you imagine? Has your experience lived up to your expectations?

. . .

AYTEN: I didn't know what it was going to be like. I met you [Sue] first, and you were really encouraging, and everyone in the company was very open and friendly. I was the youngest and smallest and the rest of them had been together for a year. I progressed a lot and my confidence and dance vocabulary expanded. For example, I didn't realise that there were so many different styles within the umbrella term of street dance. So things like popping, locking, house, hip hop, krump, breaking, tutting, etc. were all new terms for me and also new experiences. In contemporary classes we have done some Graham technique, yoga and also lifting and carrying. It has been wonderful! We have performed at places like the Royal Albert Hall, Sadler's Wells, Southbank Centre, the indigO2 and the Genée Studio at RAD Headquarters.

. . .

SUE: Has this experience influenced your plans for the future in any way?

. . .

AYTEN: Yes, in a big way because right now I want to have a career in dance and the company is preparing me well for the future because the teachers really push you. If you want to be a dancer you have to be determined and you can't slack off. So I work hard even when I am feeling tired.

. . .

SUE: Are there any other ways in which being part of the companies has made a difference to your life?

. . .

AYTEN: Yes, I feel more independent and confident – I take trains on my own now, which means my mum can stay at home!

. . .

Opposite: Step LIVE! 2013. Photo credit Foteini Christofilopoulou.

SUE: What style of dancing is your favourite and why?

…

AYTEN: I like street dance best even though it is the most tiring and exhausting. It has helped me bring out my own flavour, my own style, I can express myself. I do feel shy a lot, especially when I have to go into 'battles' – it's scary, but I'm working on it! Among all the street genres, I like house and hip hop the best. I feel I am the best at these. I have to work at popping and locking – I find this quite hard.

…

SUE: Has your family been involved in your dancing?

…

AYTEN: My parents have encouraged me to dance more. I am very lucky because many children in my culture are discouraged from dancing. My parents are very supportive. I am so lucky to have parents like that.

…

SUE: What does Step into Dance mean to you?

…

AYTEN: I have made really good friends through Step into Dance. It is like my second family. The places I have performed in have been amazing. It will look so good on my résumé. Being in the company has helped with my freestyling and choreography. It shows in my work in school.

…

SUE: Where would you like to dance?

…

AYTEN: I want to go to a dance university. I want to be like Oli [Oliver Fitzgerald is the Step into Dance Street Dance Development Officer, and runs the Street Dance Company]. I want to teach and perform – for now, that is what I want.

…

AYTEN GOKSAN
Ayten has been a member of the Step into Dance contemporary and street dance companies since 2012.

SUE GOODMAN
Sue has been teaching, performing and choreographing dance for over 30 years. She holds an MA in Dance Studies from Trinity Laban, and an MA from the Central School of Speech and Drama. Sue ran the Movement Department at Cape Town University Drama School for 5 years and then went on to found and direct South Africa's first racially integrated contemporary dance company, Jazzart, which is still in operation today.

Since settling in England, Sue has taught at Elmhurst School for Dance, The Place, Seltec, London College of Dance, the University of Winchester, and was Head of Choreography at the London Studio Centre for 10 years. For the past two decades, Sue has also taught internationally for the Royal Academy of Dance. Sue has been the Programme Artistic Director for Step into Dance, a partnership project between the Royal Academy of Dance and The Jack Petchey Foundation, since 2010.

A Hidden Curriculum: Fostering Social Cohesion in the Ballet Studio

BY HEULWEN PRICE

The reception area of a dance school on a Saturday is a hub of excitement and enthusiasm – a bustling scene of integration, a community of learning bound together by a common love of dancing. It is also a lively environment in which social education can take place.

However, education in every sense of the word, including social education, relies on appropriately educated teachers whose knowledge exceeds mere subject expertise. Viewed once again as a subject in its own right, pedagogy (teaching *how* to teach) is an essential component of high quality teacher training, and education in ballet is no exception. Whilst the main aim for children attending classes is to learn to love and to perform ballet, a well-structured class provides opportunities to learn far more: learning ballet can make a major contribution to children's social education.

Social systems are determined by fundamental needs operating within particular cultural contexts. Social roles are fluid and dynamic, and as we progress through life, we are continually inducted into differing cultural norms and values. Identifying these roles is central to development in early and teenage years as young people prepare themselves, consciously or not, for adulthood.

Social groups operate according to culturally specific rules, and harmonious integration requires an understanding of the parameters of established 'normal' behaviour. This comes about through accepting the social norms and values of the group, while at the same time maintaining awareness of one's self in relation to them.

Successful integration can thus be seen as a willingness to abide by the social code, obey instruction and to be part of a team, but, equally, to show initiative and an independent spirit. It requires freedom and the ability of the individual to make decisions. Such agency requires a fine balance between discipline, self-control, the development of the mind and freedom to experiment.

Ballet as social education for young children

Steeped in its long heritage, traditional ballet classes maintain the values handed down from the great vocational academies. On my visits to the Vaganova Academy, the Paris Opera Ballet School, and the Royal Ballet School, I observed

classes that appeared to replicate the ways in which ballet has been taught since each school's establishment. Embedded in their training is the need for self-discipline and an acceptance of rules, not only in order to develop performance and technical skills but also to live and breathe the culture of ballet. However, within these strictures there is also the need for students to build the confidence to experiment, to break out of the mould and find their own voices.

From the outside, ballet classes do not appear to be a vehicle for social development. Whilst there might be 12–15 dancers in a class, exercises are mostly performed solo. And though teacher feedback is given to the whole class, each individual student responds mostly without dialogue.

So, in what ways might ballet be seen as a contributing factor to social education?

Social and cognitive processes are not two separate functions but are reciprocal, and a well-structured and delivered pre-school ballet class ticks nearly all the boxes for social education. At this stage of learning, children demonstrate what Jean Piaget would term as 'ego-centric' characteristics (Macblain 41– 45); children are concerned with themselves while playing *alongside* rather than *with* other children.

In a pre-school ballet class, basic movement skills are often practiced by children responding to a story or an imaginative scene. You will see them following and reacting to the teacher's descriptive requests – a bit like the Pied Piper. During such classes, children have the opportunity to learn basic social skills by lining up in an orderly fashion, learning to wait their turn, and to respect personal space. Exercises which are taken *en diagonal*, for example, require that children line up and wait their own turn to perform the specific movement. Standing with arms outstretched and ensuring that no-one is touching gives youngsters the opportunity to recognise personal space. Dancing in patterns allows them to use space appropriately whilst in motion.

Slightly older children, with their increased cognition, have, in Piagetian terms, gained the ability to share or 'de-centre' (Macblain 41–45). This allows them to cope with quite complex movement patterns and, significantly, the ability to dance *with* each other – rather than *alongside* – and to share their learning experiences.

As cognition develops, so do opportunities to develop more complex social skills, and teachers are able to construct ballet classes to ensure that children achieve their dancing skills through understanding the 'what, why and how' of dancing, rather than just mimicking the movements provided. It is a false economy to teach children set ballet syllabi examination exercises without allowing time for them to actually participate in their learning and therein enable it to be deep and meaningful. Observing and imitating a teacher may achieve proficiency with simple movements, but when actions become more complex it is necessary to have sound educational models upon which to draw.

As teachers, we support learning by constantly making decisions about a child's level of achievement and what they can or need

Opposite: Photo credit Elliot Frank.

to attain. The educational precept that learning is achieved through meaningful social interaction and collaboration with others is common enough. So it makes sense for ballet teachers to adopt a similar perspective – but how?

Providing guidance and support within a collaborative environment, rather than telling a child what or what not to do, require a multiplicity of pedagogical strategies, all of which position the learner at the heart of learning. Posing questions to guide a child's thinking and focus and ensuring that they understand how new knowledge links with previous insights are just some of the tools which allow them to take on increased responsibility for managing their learning. Jerome Bruner rather imaginatively calls this 'scaffolding' (Ireson 96–99). Scaffolding provides learning support from a more experienced other (not necessarily an adult), and as learning and achievement occurs, the support or scaffold is gradually withdrawn.

Here is a vignette of how this can work in practice:

Getting the children to work on a specific topic with a partner, with one child taking the role of the teacher, allows for an exchange of ideas which promotes not only learning but also the development of social skills. Allowing children to observe each other dancing, supported with a series of well-defined questions that guide and encourage discussion, encourages them to take responsibility for their learning. Each couple can share their exploration of the topic with the group as a whole. This allows the children to have a

voice, to explore their ideas in practice and discuss the outcomes.

Engaging children through this type of collaboration, or 'reciprocal learning', also gives an opportunity for the teacher to focus on one child, whilst ensuring the other children are fully immersed in their learning. The process of sharing, listening and responding to ideas develops social skills and is easily accommodated within the ballet class.

Teachers might feel concerned that this role-sharing strategy is not the best use of class time, and that their expert knowledge is superior to that of a learner. But strong evidence shows that by getting another child to act as teacher, communication between peers may well be more advantageous than between teacher and learner (Petty 232, 364). When working amongst themselves, children will often use a common, informal language, both physical and verbal, gaining their own way of explaining and achieving often more effectively than through teacher-led instruction. By observing this dialogue, teachers can gain a real insight into the level of understanding of both the performer and the peer teacher, whilst children are also learning social integration.

Beverly Otto (19) suggests that difficulties in aural communication proficiency gives rise to different levels of achievement, as individuals who are not skilled in self-expression can by ignored by their peers. Ballet classes, however, are usually sufficiently manageable for teachers to be aware of any tensions that may arise and to dissipate awkwardness. Indeed, working

Above: Heulwin Price.

sensitively with a group of mixed-ability learners often enhances the class dynamics in a positive way, in which the development of social skills complements the enhancement of performance skills.

A similar approach can be taken when working to develop technical proficiency of a particular step. For example, children can work in pairs and provide learning support to each other rather than waiting for the teacher to tell them what and how to do the step. Having set the step within a sequence or movement phrase and allowed the children to practise it together, the following approach can be taken:

• Children get into partners
• Children decide who will be the 'child teacher'
• Following clear guidance from the teacher one child dances the movement sequence through whilst the other 'child teacher' observes
• The 'child teacher' offers feedback of the observed execution of the sequence
• Each child has the opportunity to assume the role of 'child teacher'

In encouraging peer dialogue and other collaborative approaches, teachers can support children to build upon the social skills learned at pre-school dance classes and begin to become responsible for their own learning.

Movement Analysis for the teenage dancer

Young adulthood can be an exciting but also a traumatic time. Raging hormones and the desire to test social norms and boundaries are a crucial part of the developmental process. Ballet teachers will recognise that there is something very special about teaching ballet to a group of teenagers, when one knows that many of their friends are out socialising in a very different way, and that the considerable hours that students spend in the dance studio are not necessarily undertaken with the intention of following a career in dance.

For those teenagers who continue to dance, a tight-knit social group is formed. It is during this period that they wrestle with notions about their own identity as well as explore how to be at ease within a social group. Within a friendly, secure teaching environment, they are able express their common love of ballet, as well as share secrets and explore emotions with their friends.

For RAD teachers, the Higher Grades syllabi, created specifically for teenage dancers, provides a means of facilitating a different layering of social development, explored within a context of mutual interest. Varied and quite complex channels of communication are central to the settings of these grades, where the choreographed sequences require interpretation of a wide variety of movement styles. Variations may be performed solo or with a partner, requiring students to engage with the audience through body language, eye-focus and projection of movement,

providing a means for the complexities of performance to be taken to the next stage of expectations from that of previous learning. A series of ballet steps can be beautifully executed, but unless performed with artistic and musical awareness, the choreography becomes just that: a series of steps.

Within a positive learning environment, however, teenage dancers can find their voice, both verbally and spiritually. Making use of poetry, imagery or narrative can provide a vehicle for making ballet steps meaningful. Allowing the dancers to discuss their responses and ideas, and to experiment with those ideas in movement, encourages them to share their feelings, to develop their expressive qualities, and to express their emotions in their dancing. This is what ballet performance strives to achieve, and in doing so it helps young dancers to clarify their own emotional development.

Case study

My students studying RAD Grade 8 are at the stage of exploring a variety of performance qualities and methods of communication. They have learned the choreography and now need to make something of its expressive potential.

The process that I selected provided the opportunity to explore how to give colour and appropriate dynamics to the steps. It also allowed the dancers to work with each other and with the pianist whilst I provided guidance, rather than stating what and how to perform the sequence. Developing the language of emotion allows dancers to express their own and each other's feelings, therein supporting the positive development of interpersonal relationships.

To facilitate this, we watched some DVD extracts of performances in which the interaction between the couples is central to the variation. For example, we observed James in *La Sylphide* (1832) dancing with his elusive Sylph, and the balcony *pas de deux* love scene in *Romeo and Juliet* (MacMillan 1965). The students discussed how the professional dancers use their body language to convey the narrative. This prompted the idea of each couple creating their own story through which to interpret the selected Grade 8 set choreography.

To add further colour to the movement, we considered how a 'mind-map' of word dynamics (Clunie, Dale & Paine 39) could explore and extend understanding of basic descriptive words, and therein aid the expression of ideas and emotions. We completed a chart to demonstrate how the same ballet step could be performed in a variety of ways, and discussed the range of movement dynamics and spatial patterning (including aerial and floor patterning), and how they were perceived and interpreted from the vantage point of oneself, the other dancers and the audience.

We then discussed the musical dynamics for each movement phrase. Finally, the students danced the RAD Grade 8 set choreography, imbuing it with the emotional charge of the story that they had created. For example, in the Grade 8 *Etude Lyrique* where the movement is similar to the ebb and flow of a tide, the students described in words the feeling of being pulled away from a loved one, lingering

and hesitating about returning or remaining away. The 'pull' towards and away became the central theme for the emotional performance.

Technique Class as a Conduit towards Social Development

Following a syllabus offers a clear framework but it is equally important to maintain a holistic approach to the teaching of ballet technique class to teenage students.

While the development of technical skills remains an essential part of ballet training, it should never become the dominant focus. Sound skill *is* a requirement, but without artistry and musical awareness, the dancing loses the magic that differentiates it from gymnastics.

The individual dancer needs to have some ownership and voice for their artistic performance to be meaningful: it must be part of their soul. But, with limited class time, it is understandable why teachers may resort to a didactic teaching style in which students are told what and how to perform, rather than invited to contribute to the learning process.

With careful, long-term class planning, however, an interactive and balanced approach can be maintained. Ballet teachers can vary the delivery of technique training so that some classes or sections of a class will necessarily continue to be predominantly teacher led, while others can facilitate the development of artistic and musical elements through social interaction. A class dominated by 'teacher talk' offering technical analysis and feedback on the performance of specific steps, for instance, can

be followed by a class designed to allow more emphasis on the student's voice.

One approach might be to use two pieces of music contrasting in *tempi*, style or even varying time signatures, to perform the same sequence. Students can then discuss the qualities of each piece of music and how they influence their execution of the movement sequences, both from a technical and artistic perspective. In inviting the students to share their reactions, the teacher may get the dialogue rolling in order to encourage students who are less confident in sharing ideas with adults, or indeed openly with peers. Pairing or grouping students for further discussion can also serve as a kind of mentoring process, in which the students feel emboldened to reveal to their peers what might be quite personal observations.

Discussion can extend to include the 'colouring' of the music and movement. Highlighting *staccato* and *legato* sounds, *crescendo*, *pianissimo* and varying *tempi* within the piece, for instance, draws attention to how the punctuation of the music can be expressed through the ballet performance. It is essential to establish a positive, supportive and non-judgemental environment, as each student may well hear, feel and relate to these experiences in a very different manner. Students should be further encouraged to express why they feel or interpret words and movements as they do, and teachers must take care to be very positive in their responses, even if the student's

Above: Heulwin Price and students at the RAD conference.

interpretation differs from their own. Such teaching strategies inspire young dancers to overcome inhibitions by enhancing their capacity to communicate both verbally and bodily, and therein help ensure the dancing will come from the soul rather than be externally clothed (and sometimes rather ill-fitting).

Providing space in class plans to incorporate student participation is, in my experience, an extremely effective means to improve performance. Knowing one's students' make-up allows teachers to respond more personally to each individual. Gaining insights into students' ideas and emotions regarding how dancing informs their sense of self, will contribute towards the creation of a warm, secure environment that allows all dance students to develop confidence and self-esteem.

Dancing is social, and ballet classes are no exception. Ballet can and does provide a rigorous, inspiring and transformative means of social education.

References

Clunie, Maggie, Liz Dale, and Lyn Paine. *AQA GCSE Dance*. Cheltenham: Nelson Thornes Ltd., 2009. Print.

Ireson, Judith. *Learners, Learning and Educational Activity*. Oxon: Routledge, 2008. Print.

Macblain, Sean. *How Children Learn*. London: Sage, 2014. Print.

Otto, Beverly. *Language Development in Early Childhood*. 4th ed. Pearson: 2014. Print.

Petty, Geoff. *Teaching Today*. Fourth Edition. Cheltenham: Nelson Thomas, 2009. Print.

RAD. *Graded Examinations in Dance: Grade 8, Female Syllabus*. London: Royal Academy of Dance, 2006. Print.

HEULWEN PRICE

Drawing on experience gained from a professional performing career as well as extensive international teaching, Heulwen is a member of the Faculty of Education at the Royal Academy of Dance, specialising in teacher education in dance and specifically in ballet. She currently teachers young children and students ballet and is responsible for Performance and Teaching Studies for the Undergraduate and Master's Programmes. She also supports the delivery of the RAD Professional Awards to the international dance community.

Heulwen has written teaching programmes for dance pedagogy and mentoring and has explored extensively the educational opportunities that children and students gain from learning ballet. She was a member of the creative team that created the RAD Graded Syllabi (1991) and tutors all the recently launched new RAD syllabi both in the UK and at international dance centres. An Examiner for the RAD, Heulwen coaches and teaches both syllabi and non-syllabi classes.

Tending the Spirit: Spiritual Wellbeing through Dance

BY PAMELA ALEXANDER

I praise the dance,
for it frees people from the heaviness
    of matter
and binds the isolated to community.

I praise the dance, which demands everything:
health and a clear spirit and a buoyant soul.

Dance is a transformation of space, of time,
    of people,
who are in constant danger of becoming
    all brain,
will, or feeling.

Dancing demands a whole person,
one who is firmly anchored in the center
    of his life,
who is not obsessed by lust for people and things
and the demon of isolation in his own ego.

Dancing demands a freed person,
one who vibrates with the equipoise
    of all his powers.

I praise the dance.

O man, learn to dance,
or else the angels in heaven will not know
    what to do with you.

Attributed to Augustine of Hippo (354–430 AD)

Some of us may be wondering what the spiritual dimension has to do with dance. Others may view spirituality as inherent in their practice without giving it much thought. Spirituality, however, is an essential aspect of being human, and experts are calling for raised awareness of it across the teaching profession. I address it under four broad headings: *What is spirituality? Spirituality and Education, Why dance?* and *Tending the Spirit.*

What is spirituality?

Spirituality is hard to define. In postmodern society, any definition has to be acceptable to people of all faiths and none, and has therefore emerged from under the religious umbrella to be interpreted and expressed in multiple and diverse ways. In contemporary culture, it seems to act as a kind of signpost, indicating that people have a need to live with a sense of meaning, value and mystery (Lynch 105).

My search for enlightenment has led me to contemplate diverse interpretations. A common thread seems to be that spiritual awareness is a conduit to sensing the connections within oneself, with others, with the world, and with 'Other' – the awareness that the self is not the

centre of the universe (Ashley 122; Blain & Eady 127). I found anything spiritual is grounded both in the relational aspects of being human and in the integration of the 'whole being'. The kind of relationships we are talking about are relationship with self (self-awareness), relationship with another, relationships among people, relationship with both place and things (spatial), and relationship with transcendence, that is 'God', 'the Cosmos' or other 'Higher Being'. These dimensions should all be understood as belonging together in an integrated whole (Lartey 141).

Melanie Purdy and Peggy Dupey, who devised the Holistic 'Flow' Model of Spiritual Wellness, suggest that spirituality is not something static and definable, but a 'flow of energy' that allows individuals to be active in all dimensions of life. Spiritual 'flow' is a state of total involvement in an activity that requires complete concentration. Involvement is so intense that it transcends conscious thought – one literally becomes lost in the satisfaction of one's activity (Csikszentmihalyi 1999, cited in Purdy and Dupey 98). Teachers of the performing arts have a special advantage in being able to bring heightened (spiritual) awareness to the classroom (Suhor 16), because "all the arts engage the heart as well as the intellect" (Carr 1995, 96).

In terms of lifelong wellbeing, it is widely recognised and has been agreed upon across healthcare professions for many years, that "health is not just the absence of disease; it is a balanced state of physical, psychological, and spiritual wellbeing" (World Health Organisation, cited in Spencer 1). And, like a faithful couple, "spirituality and health are bonded to each other, inseparable companions, in the dance of joy and sadness, health and illness, birth and death" (Wright, cited in Spencer 5).

Spirituality and education

The primary concern of education is education of the 'whole being'. This is usually taken to include spiritual, moral, social and cultural (SMSC) development, where teaching extends beyond coaching or training to a wider personal formation (Carr 2003, 45 & 47). Furthermore, experts in the UK agree that *all* National Curriculum subjects should provide opportunities to promote pupils' SMSC, putting it "at the very heart of every subject we teach" (Scherer 1991, cited in Crossman 511). As such, Spiritual Education has had legal status in schools in the UK since 1944 (Eaude 2008, 6–7).

Meanwhile, in 1989, The United Nations Convention on the Rights of the Child legislated for the child's voice to be heard in a variety of arenas. Despite these measures and the legal status of SMSC, however, childrens' spiritual voices are not always being heard. While concepts of SMSC may overlap, the spiritual has distinctive qualities which probe at a deeper level, and which are easily neglected as teachers focus on delivering a substantial curriculum and meeting targets (Adams 103, 115). A further two significant reasons for marginalisation of spiritual education in the public sector have been identified:

First is the association of spirituality with religion. While many people do indeed find religion a path towards developing and expressing spirituality, spiritual development can occur quite apart from it (Trousdale, cited in Baumgartner and Buchanan). To that end, attention to our spiritual side must be for everyone, religious or not.

Second, although spirituality is widespread it has become privatised. During a period of research involving the spiritual experience of adults, Professor David Hay found that many adults are shy of talking about their spirituality for fear of being ridiculed. In turn children pick up on this and choose not to reveal their spiritual experiences in case they are not taken seriously (Hay and Nye 30, 127). This is a pity because children are capable of making profound spiritual responses and we need to be open and alert to them.

Attention to the spiritual is important not only as a legal aim of education, but because of the way it enriches teaching and learning. It helps children to grow and develop as people by developing the knowledge, skills, understanding, qualities and attitudes, to foster their own inner lives and non-material wellbeing (DforE [online], HMI). But where does the responsibility for this lie?

Traditionally, the nurture of our spiritual side has been the responsibility of ministers of religion. Whilst that is still very much the case, large numbers of people no longer belong to a faith community. In the UK, because of the legal status of spiritual education and the emphasis on whole person education, and in order to embrace all cultures, all faiths (and none), attention to the spiritual now lies heavily at the door of teachers – of all kinds. This is also increasingly the case for teachers across the international education sector.

Teachers of dance are very much concerned for the overall wellbeing of their pupils but they might not see the spiritual dimension as pertaining to them. Whilst SMSC is not identified as a prerequisite of specialist teachers in the private sector, dance teachers nonetheless play a key role in the lives of the people they teach. In school, the children have a new class teacher every year. Because of this, very often the dance teacher gives continuity throughout a child's formative years when all about them is changing.

Like teachers in schools, however, many private sector dance teachers wrestle with performance outcomes and exam results. In that process, many may miss opportunities to nurture spiritual development. But by not addressing spirituality, educators are not fully responding to the notion of the whole child (Adams 119). In order to tend the spirit of those in our care, some degree of spiritual knowledge is widely deemed crucial for culturally competent practice, especially for those for whom spirituality is a salient part of their lives (Hodge & Dezerotes 112). To that end, experts consider it timely to investigate or reconnect with our own attitudes, beliefs and values about the spiritual dimension, which can be surprisingly enriching (Fraser & Grootenboer 308).

Why Dance?

Like the spiritual, dance is grounded in the relational. It is also capable of integrating all that it is to be human: the physical, intellectual, spiritual, emotional, social, moral, cultural and creative. It invites 'whole person' involvement, which is the agent for spiritual 'flow'. According to theologian JG Davies, dance engages the mind, body and intellect; the dancer is his or her own instrument of dance expression – *the dancer* – not the body as some object other than the performer (97). In other words, at the moment of movement, the dancer *is* the *arabesque* or the *pirouette* and so forth; he or she, the person, is not separate from it. Dance is also capable of crossing the boundaries of faith, ability, culture and language and of penetrating the soul at a level often inexpressible in words "revelatory knowledge is direct, deeply emotional and inarticulate" (Wosien 11). It caters for diverse spiritualties too, which I will come to, but first, a word of caution.

The individualistic and consumerist life-style of the West pervades both the education system and the arts world. Children are motivated to learn, by emphasising the need to get on in life, where 'getting on' is understood in terms of high salary and material possessions (Halstead 5). Although spirituality continues to express itself strongly in the realm of the arts, the message is easily missed. For Hay, the arts as a whole are reduced to being a commodity providing diversion or entertainment and their spiritual power is diluted or lost (with Nye 44). Materialism, mechanism, unbridled competition and individualism, are forces in our culture that work against the spiritual flourishing of children and adults alike (Wilson 25).

Dance in the curriculum of many countries has long been regarded as physical activity, with the emphasis on skill, competition, and health and fitness at the expense of expression and artistry. Some private dance studios, though not all, are driven by preparation for exams and shows, with a resulting emphasis on the product rather than the process: the success of the business depends on it. How then are we to address emerging spiritualties in the classroom or studio?

Tending the Spirit

In a guide for all who work in healthcare, Stephen Spencer explains that spirituality is about who we are, our identity, the very essence of self. At the deepest core of who we are as human beings, we have three fundamental needs: for security – a need to belong, to be cared for, to be loved, to be valued as a unique individual; for self-worth – a need to feel good about ourselves; and for significance – a need to have a sense of meaning or purpose, that our lives really count, that we are respected and that our contribution is worthwhile (2).

Our spiritual needs are being met when we are being listened to, being affirmed and valued, being respected, given emotional support and being understood. It follows then, that we can help students in the same way that we ourselves would be helped: by listening to them properly, by affirming and valuing them as unique human beings, by showing respect,

by giving emotional support, by empathising, and by giving access to religious support if appropriate (Spencer 4).

Spirituality is not a 'teachable' concept and so there is no discrete curriculum to support it in the classroom. Whilst we cannot plan and predict precisely what will foster spirituality in classroom or studio, we can, however, cultivate a climate that enhances it. A spiritually safe classroom is one in which healthy exploration and discussion can take place in a non-judgmental, non-self-conscious environment (Fraser and Grootenboer 307). In a multi-faith or non-faith context, the spiritual autonomy of individuals is recognised and any resources that inspire and engage individuals at a deeper level are drawn upon. In addition, knowledge of spiritual identities and what spiritual experience might entail, equips teachers to recognise and grasp opportunities for tending the spirit when they arise.

Spiritual identity cuts across religious affiliation and can be expressed in multiple and interconnected ways. Researchers suggest that the following approaches may be implemented in all areas of the curriculum:

- **Socio-centric** where some feel a sense of good in helping others
- **Eco-centric** where others feel a connection to nature
- **Cosmo-centric** where others feel a sense of awe and wonder at the cosmos
- **Geneo-centric** where some show deep feelings for their ancestors

- **Senso-centric** where others are moved by a beautiful piece of art or by listening to certain kinds of music
- **Chrono-centric** still others feel spiritual experience in relation to time such as significant events, and
- **Transo-centric** where some express their spirituality in social or ecological contexts inspired by their connection to a divine source. (Kirmani and Kirmani 378–381).

Knowledge of these identities can heighten our own spiritual awareness and, in a dance context, provide starting points for creative work.

Spiritual experience entails a sense of awe and wonder, reflective silence, play and delight (Eaude 2005, 246). It may also include a heightened sense of energy or vitality, a sense of belonging, and an affinity with mystery (Claxton, cited in Fraser and Grootenboer 309). Delight is most likely to be displayed or experienced as dance educators lead students through valuable movement journeys from the mechanically correct to expressive movement (Kretchemar, cited in Lodewyk et al 176).

The spontaneous nature of spiritual experience means that teachers need to be prepared for an element of surprise. Insight-glimpsing experiences in the classroom might well entail a spontaneous laugh, grunt or grin, a well turned, often metaphorical, phrase, a thoughtful statement that surprises even the speaker, a pleased or troubled glance, an excitedly raised hand, or an inarticulate attempt at orally formulating an insight. For many, witnessing such moments of enlightened growth is one of the greatest pleasures of teaching (Suhor 15–16).

Looking at the teaching environment, planning, interaction and assessment through a spiritual lens offers new and creative ways of enriching the experience and self-understanding of both students and teachers (Eaude 2005, 247). If we see ourselves as agents of joy and conduits of transcendence, rather than merely as licensed trainers or coaches, or promoters of measurable growth, then spirituality may flourish in the classroom (Suhor 15–16). Furthermore, an active spirituality can bring increasing liberation from the anxiety, pace, addictions and performance-based self-worth inherent in many mainstream lifestyles, which must be of value to children and teachers alike (Daly, cited in Lodewyk et al). Is it possible that, in turn, adopting a more spiritual approach in dance classes might ultimately lead to improved overall performance and examination results? Perhaps a few observations gleaned from my work with the Education Department at Rochester Cathedral may offer insights for dance teachers as to how the nurturing of spirituality might work in practice.

In 2009, just after I enrolled on the RAD's Master of Teaching Dance (MTD), I was invited to work on a collaborative project (The Calming of the Storm) in which children with special educational needs could explore their spirituality in the Cathedral space, using dance. The children devised movements that told the story of a storm and were encouraged to share their responses to the experience. These ranged from 'feeling frightened' when the storm was at its height, to gratitude when it had subsided. In a creative class with my Grade 3 ballet pupils during the trial period, one child said, "before it was just a story, but it felt like it really was a storm", while another said, "I could actually feel the sea spray on my face… I could even hear Jesus snoring." Teachers' evaluations of the project showed that the exercise was a rich means of implementing dance as a 'tool' for exploring space, spirituality and heritage, and that it helped some of them to address their difficulty in responding to the profound, spiritual observations made by children visiting the Cathedral.

Such encouragement for children to express their spirituality has not, unfortunately, always transpired at the Cathedral, which welcomes over 15,000 school children each year. The Saint Luke window, for instance, which features a purple bull representing Jesus as a royal sacrifice, prompted one child to note, "purple is the colour of a bruise, could it mean that we have a bruised soul before knowing Jesus?" The Cathedral's Education Officer recalls that the child's teacher tutted, rolled her eyes, and shook her head. Happily, a member of the education team was present to affirm the child's comment, and therein avert the silencing of another spiritual voice.

Within a dance class context, the key for teachers is to similarly establish an open and non-judgmental ambience, in which the spiritual dimension of the childrens' response to movement is neither stifled nor ridiculed, but rather embraced as a natural aspect of their dance experience. A heightened spiritual awareness means a heightened awareness of self, sense of belonging, sense of relationship with others and a sense of something or someone greater or 'other' than oneself. The art of dance generates a sense of wellbeing, which I suggest, is due to the state of balance engendered by integration of the whole being through the total involvement that allows the spirit to 'flow'. And, grounded in the relational, it 'bucks the trend' that has privatised spirituality.

To treat all children from a holistic perspective is, in the long run, to treat the whole of society. If teachers of all kinds are spiritually aware, then the spiritual voice of children will be restored to them and remain with them throughout adulthood. That dance is a major contributor to overall physical, psychological and spiritual wellbeing is not a new phenomenon, as Augustine of Hippo attests.

References

Adams, Kate. "The rise of the child's voice; the silencing of the spiritual Voice". *Journal of Beliefs and Values* 30.2 (2009): 113–122. Print.

Ashley, Martin. "Spiritual, Moral and Cultural Development". *Improving Teaching and Learning in the Humanities.* Ed. Martin Ashley. London: Falmer. 1999. Print.

Baumgartner, Jennifer J. and Teresa Buchanan. "Supporting Each Child's Spirit". *Young Children* March (2010): 90–95. Print.

Blain, Mary and Sandra Eady. "The WOW factor: spiritual development through Science". *Westminster Studies in Education* 25.2 (2002): 125–135. Print.

Carr, David. "Towards a distinctive conception of spiritual education". *Oxford Review of Education* 21.1 (1995): 83–98. Print.

---. *Making Sense of Education*. Oxon: Routledge, 2003. Print.

Crossman, Joanna. "Secular Spiritual Development in Education from International and Global Perspectives". *Oxford Review of Education* 29.4 (2003): 503–520. Print.

Davies, John G. *Liturgical Dance: An Historical, Theological and Practical Handbook*. London: SCM Press Ltd, 1984. Print.

Department for Education. Web. 8 Oct. 2010. www.education.gov.uk

Eaude, Tony. "Strangely familiar? – Teachers making sense of young children's spiritual development". *Early Years* 25.3 (2005): 237–248. Print.

---. *Children's Spiritual, Moral, Social and Cultural Development*. Exeter: Learning Matters Ltd, 2008. Print.

Fraser, Deborah and Peter Grootenboer. "Nurturing spirituality in secular classrooms". *International Journal of Children's Spirituality*. 9.3 (2004): 307–320. Print.

Halstead, J. Mark. Guest Editorial *International Journal of Children's Spirituality*. 4.1 (1999): 5–7. Print.

Hay, David and Rebecca Nye. *The Spirit of the Child*. London: Jessica Kingsley Publishers, 2006. Print.

HMI: Ofsted 2004 "Promoting and evaluating pupils' spiritual, moral, social and cultural development: Office for Standards in Education". 9 Oct. 2010. www.ofsted.gov.uk/resources/promoting-and-evaluating-pupils-spiritual-moral-social-and-cultural-development

Hodge, David and David Dezerotes. "Postmodernism and Spirituality: Some Pedagogical Implications for Teaching Content on Spirituality". *Journal of Social Work Education*. 44.1 (2008): 103–123. Print.

Kirmani, Mubina and Sanaullah Kirmani. "Recognition of seven spiritual identities and its implications on children". *International Journal of Children's Spirituality*. 14.4 (2009): 369–383. Print.

Lartey, Emmanual Y. *In Living Colour: an intercultural approach to pastoral care and counselling*. London: Jessica Kingsley Publishers, 2003. Print.

Lodewyk, Ken, Chunlie Lu and Jeanne Kentel. "Enacting the Spiritual Dimension in Physical Education". *Physical Educator*. 66.40 (2009): 170–179. Print.

Lynch, Gordon. *After Religion: 'Generation X' and the search for meaning*. London: Dartman, Longman and Todd Ltd, 2002. Print.

Meehan, Christopher. "Promoting Spiritual Development in the Curriculum". *Pastoral Care* March (2002):16–24. Print.

Purdy, Melanie and Peggy Dupey. "Holistic Flow Model of Spiritual Wellness". *Counselling and Values* 49 (2005): 95–106. Print.

Spencer, Steven. *Spiritual Care: a guide for all who work in Healthcare*. Medway NHS Foundation Trust, 2012. Print.

Suhor, Christopher. "Spirituality – Letting it grow in the classroom". *Educational Leadership* Dec 98 –Jan 99 (1999): 12–16. Print.

Wilson, Ruth. "The Spiritual Life of Children". *Wellness and Nature* September – October (2010):24–27. Print.

Wosien, Gabrielle. *Sacred Dance*. USA: Thames and Hudson, 1974. Print.

PAMELA ALEXANDER

Pamela Alexander – Master of Teaching (Dance), BA (Hons), BPhil (Hons) – has taught ballet for more than forty years, both freelance and as Principal of the Rochester School of Ballet. Pam is ordained in the Church of England where she is as much an advocate for the use of dance in nurturing spirituality, both in school and in church, as she is for raising spiritual awareness across the teaching profession. In addition to her parish duties, Pam undertakes sessional teaching for the Education Department at Rochester Cathedral, teaches Theology to the Apprentices of Springs Dance Company, and has academic responsibility for the Creative and Expressive Arts in Mission and Ministry module for the Licensed Lay Ministry programme in the Diocese of Rochester. Pam is a Life Member of the Royal Academy of Dance.

In Conversation: Dance United Performance Company member Charles and Haris Marathefti

Founded in 2000, Dance United creates bespoke dance projects and interventions aimed at transforming the lives of marginalized people. The opportunities it offers to gain experience in contemporary dance training and, for those who wish to continue this training, to join its performance companies, has fostered positive change for many young people and adults. These include gang members, youth offenders, and others struggling with mental illness, addictions, and seriously challenging behaviours.

As per Dance United's protocols, we cite the dancer, Charles, by his first name only.

Charles approached Dance United after hearing about the company when visiting the Rathbone Centre – a jobs and training centre in Hackney, London. At the time, Charles was homeless and completely impoverished, with no support from his family, charities, or statutory service providers.

…

HARIS: Have you always loved to dance?

…

CHARLES: I was brought up being told dance was wrong and that it was a barrier instead of a pathway. That it would stop me from achieving and accomplishing things in my life. But I've been dancing secretly my whole life and to this day, my blood family has no clue of what it is I do.

…

HARIS: How did your journey with Dance United begin?

…

CHARLES: The journey started when I joined the Dance United cohort – this was around the same time as the 2011 riots. I remember being outside and there was a woman going around the streets and she was stopping individuals and talking to them about partnerships and what they wanted to do. Obviously, it was a crazy day for a lot of young people, but I spoke with her, and she told me about a building, right around the corner from where I live, known as Rathbone.

When I went to Rathbone I met a guy who kinda spoke to me on a one to one basis, and he asked me, "What's your passion? What do you like?" I mentioned dance to him and, to my surprise, after two weeks he called me and told me that I'd had an email from Dance United. I went to Rathbone and we went over the email, and it had a contact at Dance United. I called them and they let me know that there was a taster day that week. All I can remember

Opposite: Dance United performance. Photo credit Pari Nader.

is just being at that taster day and I haven't looked back ever since.

…

HARIS: What was your first day in Dance United like?

…

CHARLES: The night before I was over-excited. It's just one of those feelings you get, like you are entering this new dimension, this new world. You're saying goodbye to the old you. I didn't really sleep much, but I was one of the first people there the next day, which was the taster day. We got to make smoothies and then dance, and once we went into the studio, everyone just clicked. I felt like I knew everyone from before.

So, the first day went really well – everyone got to know each other, we made jokes, we worked together, we understood a bit about each other. Some people were very quiet, but I'm an open person – I'm just bubbly and friendly, so I was running up to everyone, saying, "Hi, my name is Charles, what's your name?" Yeah, that was my first day with the cohort.

…

HARIS: What did you observe about other people's journeys in your cohort?

…

CHARLES: I did make close friends with people, like my mate, John. I worked with him quite a bit in the studio and as the journey went on, I realised that sometimes I would get stuck and turn to him for help, and sometimes he'd get stuck and I'd try to encourage him to carry on with his work. He always used to get frustrated and I'd be, like, "Come on man, you're better

than this." I used to try and encourage him, but sometimes I realised I couldn't and that's when I saw that everyone has their own boundaries and levels of concentration in what they can do and can't do.

That's when I also realised that my journey isn't going to be the same as everyone else's. And from then on, especially after my first performance at the South Bank for my graduation, I realised that I wanted to make sure that I really stood out.

…

HARIS: What happened when the training period ended?

…

CHARLES: After we graduated we had a little party – everyone exchanged contacts and stuff like that. The main thing that I wanted to come back for was the Performance Company. We were told about it during the training and we knew we had to audition for it, but we didn't get to audition until we came back in January 2012. Now I'm a part of the Performance Company.

…

HARIS: What would you say to someone who's never heard of Dance United but is thinking about dance training?

…

CHARLES: Take the first step and just come in, seriously. It's very hard to say this, but I realised that if I didn't get up and do it, then I was just going to be at home, sleeping and eating … I wouldn't want to get up for a whole week. Now I've realised that the first step to – not so much being successful, but to being ambitious, is just that – taking that first step.

I never had anyone to say, "Come on man, just go and find something. Just pick up a book, a pen, or something." Those of you who don't know Dance United, well, just go into Google and type 'dance'. Research it.

…

HARIS: Has your experience with Dance United, and now being in the Performance Company, had an impact on your longer term goals?

…

CHARLES: I've never had a long term goal before Dance United. I look at my life and have nothing to show for it but crime. One bad choice can ruin your life. I started with one good choice that led to other good choices – looking for something to do and making some changes with my life, instead of staying at home, dwelling on my past, smoking to block out most of the pain and questions … of living a lonely life.

At the time, I never realised it, but my God had answered my prayers. I came into contact with Dance United and for the first time in my life, well, Dance United was, and is, the best thing that's happened. At times when my world felt like it was on fire, I was allowed to express my feeling and emotions in what I now know is the best way possible. I was able to dance with the flames. Dance United taught me how to turn that anger and rage into movement and gave me my space, a 'stage'. What I've learned, while being around Dance United, is that if you want something in life, you have to be prepared to fight for it. This is me fighting for it.

Thank you, Dance United.

CHARLES
Charles joined the Dance United Academy project in 2011, and dedicated himself wholeheartedly to his dance training. Upon completing the Dance United Academy programme, he was referred to Hackney Community College and accepted into Dance United's London Performance Company. It soon became apparent that Charles was not only a tremendously talented dancer, but also a very good leader. He has consistently supported and encouraged his fellow dancers to attempt the same levels of achievement he strives for himself. He has performed at Dance United and other high profile events, working with some of the most accomplished contemporary choreographers in the UK.

HARIS MARATHEFTI
Haris trained at London Studio Centre and graduated with a BA Hons Degree in Theatre Dance in 2006. She continued her studies at Birkbeck University of London, gaining a Diploma and a Masters in Arts Management while undertaking the Certificate in Ballet Teaching Studies (CBTS) at the Royal Academy of Dance and qualifying as a registered RAD teacher. Haris began working for Dance United in 2009, and was Dance United Performance Company Director from September 2011 to July 2014.

Getting Physical: Practical Approaches to Dance Anatomy

BY JANINE STREULI

Over the last few decades the dance world has placed ever growing emphasis on health, fitness and wellbeing to ensure safe practice, peak performance and longer lasting careers. In 1996, the first Dance UK *Fit to Dance?* report suggested that dancers and teachers should know more about how the body works (Brinson & Dick 151) and that all students in training should learn anatomy as applied to dance (152). Almost a decade later in 2005, the *Fit to Dance 2* report suggested that dance teachers still needed to be encouraged to do more to keep their anatomical knowledge up to date (Laws 100).

Thanks to organisations such as the International Association of Dance Medicine and Science (IADMS), Dance UK and many others, much progress has been made in the field of dance medicine and science so that information is now much more readily available for teachers, students and professional dancers. Nowadays, academic dance qualifications such as undergraduate degrees and the Dance A-Level (AQA) include a considerable amount of dance anatomy, making it more vital than ever that dance teachers "possess a solid basis of anatomical knowledge that they can

communicate in an accessible and effective way in the classroom." (Vogel 50).

Are dance teachers, however, really equipped to do this? The number of accessible and inclusive dance anatomy publications is sparse and there are even fewer that address how to teach dance anatomy. To help redress the dearth of teaching resources, this piece proposes an innovative, resource-based dance anatomy teaching model, which makes use of recent innovations in medical education and the concept of Problem Based Learning.

Firstly, we will identify the main challenges that are associated with the teaching and learning of dance anatomy. This is followed by a discussion of a dance anatomy teaching model, which was created by applying principles from medical anatomy education. The detailed discussion of the teaching model frequently refers to resources that help illustrate how dance anatomy teaching might manifest itself.

The challenges

Unsurprisingly, anatomical terminology is a big challenge as students consider it "loads of weird long words that we don't understand" (research participant). Therefore teachers need to provide plenty of opportunities for students to practise, repeat and apply the terminology.

The second challenge arises from the nature of dance anatomy resources, the length and complexity of which are often unsuitable for students with little anatomical experience. The nature of the visual materials within many established publications can also be inhibiting as they contain fairly few (and mostly black and white) illustrations.

Thirdly, anatomy is too easily perceived as 'science' and some dance students can be intimidated by that. Many choose the subject because of their interest in artistic, creative and practical work. As such, it can be a challenge to include and then motivate the less scientifically inclined individuals in the learning of dance anatomy.

The fourth and final challenge discussed here lies within the theory-practice dichotomy that is so unhelpful when attempting to develop an embodied understanding of a subject like dance anatomy. In many dance curricula, such as the UK's current A-Level (AQA), dance anatomy is assessed in writing and therefore it is all too easy to pigeonhole the subject as 'theory'.

To overcome all these challenges, teaching really needs to enable students to see the relevance of anatomy in all aspects of dance education. Especially given the sparsely available research into dance anatomy, effective teaching needs to cater for multiple learning styles (Daniels 94). Experiential learning of anatomy within technique classes, for example, can help

make the subject non-threatening (Salk 97) and incorporating "somatic practices is a good first step toward integration of body and mind" (Pengelly 79) when learning anatomy.

Medical anatomy education

As there are very few dance-specific publications on the subject of teaching anatomy, approaches used within the medical sector seemed to be a suitable place to look for solutions. Problem Based Learning (PBL) has been increasingly used as a teaching method in medical anatomy since the 1970s (Davies and Harden 130). Nowadays, the PBL approach is endorsed by many leading medical schools and the UK General Medical Council (GMC 11).

PBL combines multiple scientific subjects into real life clinical problems, as opposed to teaching each subject in isolation (Drake 475). It is a student-centred educational approach (Davis & Harden 132), which emphasises active rather than passive learning (Drake 475) by providing problem solving exercises as a starting point (Rizzolo et al. 142). So it seemed that a similar integrated teaching approach could potentially help a great deal to overcome the challenges associated with learning dance anatomy.

Before explaining the proposed teaching model, I want to explore how students can benefit from learning anatomy via PBL. At this point, I need to emphasise that there is a lot of medical research available on this topic so we can only really scratch the surface.

The group processes inherent in PBL develop problem solving skills in students

(Percac & Goodenough 203) so that they learn how and what to learn, and avoid mere regurgitation of facts (Xu 6). In this way, PBL promotes efficient memorisation processes (Yiou & Goodenough 193) that boost long-term retention (Rizzolo 1; El Moamly 189). It gives students a strong foundation of knowledge which "prepares them to assimilate a lifetime of new anatomical information" (Rizzolo 151). Several studies reveal that student motivation can be boosted by PBL (Drake 478; El Moamly 189; Anyaehie et al. 117) so that attendance and participation improve as a consequence (Anyaehie et al. 117). Research has also shown that active participation helps students recognise the holistic nature of situations so that they can better recognise the complementary nature of theory and practice (Becker et al. 57).

These findings from medical literature clearly suggest that PBL can address most of the dance anatomy challenges identified earlier. The transferable and key skills, in particular, can also help develop the study skills that students require at higher education level whilst at the same time addressing general educational initiatives and objectives.

The proposed teaching model

The teaching model that lies at the heart of this paper is illustrated in Fig. 1. An important feature is the arrow on the left hand side which indicates that this is a range of eight teaching methods and is not intended as a linear path. Its flexibility allows teachers to combine any number of methods from any area within the spectrum to use in conjunction with PBL. Each method is explained (below) and illustrated with reference to practical examples.

Methods used in conjunction with PBL

Fig. 1: Dance Anatomy Teaching Model

Anatomy Theory

Illustrations/handouts Use of high quality colour illustrations on handouts

Models Skeleton, joint models, real objects (e.g. chicken bones/joints)

Manipulation (simulation) Plasticene to build models and muscles; therabands to simulate muscle movement on the skeleton

E-learning www.getbodysmart.com (Sheffield), *Interactive Functional Anatomy* (Hillman), *Muscle System Pro III* (3D4Medical) and anatomy apps

Repertoire Identifying anatomical principles during appreciation and performance of dance repertoire

Somatic practice For example: Pilates, yoga, improvisation, visualisation, imagery, relaxation, etc.

Technique Focusing on anatomical principles during technique class to facilitate anatomically correct and informed technique

Choreography Choreographic tasks based on anatomy

Dance Practice

Fig. 2: Example handout – the structure and function of the spine

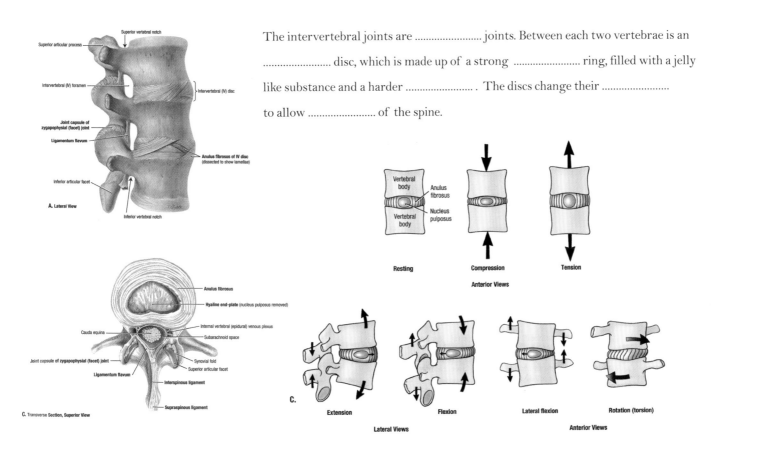

The intervertebral joints are .... joints. Between each two vertebrae is an .... disc, which is made up of a strong .... ring, filled with a jelly like substance and a harder .... The discs change their .... to allow .... of the spine.

Illustrations and handouts

Colour illustrations on accessible handouts are vital to support the learning and retention process. The example handout on the spine (Fig. 2) illustrates a conducive layout with a relatively small amount of text in favour of images that detail the structure and texture of the spine on the left hand side and its basic function on the right. To engage students in the PBL process, they are required to complete the missing words in the text by themselves, a process that also helps familiarise them with key anatomical terminology (the missing words in this example are: cartilaginous, intervertebral, fibrous, core, shape, movement). It is crucial that any handouts are visually appealing to revisit and revise from and it is worth noting that all images in Fig. 2 were obtained from non-dance sources.

Fig. 2: Agur, Anne M. R., and Arthur F. Dalley. *Grant's Atlas of Anatomy.* Twelfth Edition. Philadelphia: Wolters Kluwer Health/Lippincott Williams & Wilkins, 2009. Print. 304, 305 & 307.

Models

The use of anatomical models can help students contextualise the images on any handouts in relation to the body's three-dimensional structure. The model of the spine and pelvis in Fig. 3, for example, shows the different texture of the discs and bones and can highlight the function of the spine through manual manipulation beyond the illustrations on the example handout (Fig. 2).

Nowadays, such models can be bought cheaply from a range of online retailers (including Amazon) and their shelf life and educational potential is considerable.

Fig. 3: Model of the pelvis and spine

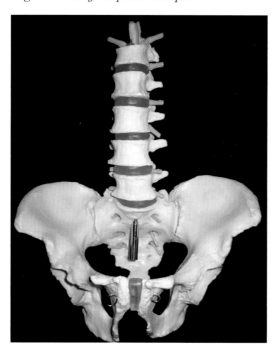

Fig. 3, 4, 5 & 7: Photographs by Janine Streuli

Manipulation

The method of manipulation requires each learner's tactile involvement with anatomical principles, as illustrated here via two further practical tasks. Students examine an image of a synovial joint, then work in small groups and use different coloured Plasticene to make a three-dimensional model of the joint and its structural components (Fig. 4). This activity aims to help them contextualise a two-dimensional illustration of a synovial joint within the body's three-dimensional structure and it often proves to be more challenging than first meets the eye. Once the models are created, peer assessment can lead to interesting debates which often help students clarify their understanding of how the joint is structured.

Fig. 4: Plasticene joint models closed and open (below)

Fig. 5: Foot skeleton with a selection of intrinsic foot muscles made of Plasticene

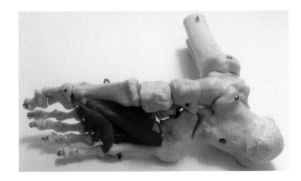

Another task, combing the methods of models and manipulation, requires the student to use the skeletal model of the foot and Plasticene to build the various layers of the intrinsic foot muscles (Fig. 5). The muscle models are not intended to be perfect in minute detail. Rather, it is hoped that the activity illustrates to the students how complex and intricate these muscles are, especially so in relation to their role in elevation, shock absorption and *pointe* work.

Plasticene can be purchased online, from arts and crafts and toy shops.

E-learning

A major challenge associated with the learning of dance anatomy lies in the fact that much of what we study is hidden inside the body. Recent developments in technology, however, have made it possible to gain access to resources that help to circumvent this challenge. Software such as *Interactive Functional Anatomy* (Hillman) and apps like *Muscle System Pro III* (3D4Medical) or the website www.getbodysmart.com allow

users to interact with muscle illustrations and animations in a range of ways. Some applications are rather expensive, yet very comprehensive, and allow users to access a detailed interior, X-ray type view from many different angles to gain an understanding of what goes on deep inside the body (Hillman) while others are reasonably priced and easily brought into the classroom on tablet devices (3D4Medical).

One advantage of the website www.getbodysmart.com is that it relates the function of the muscle to the whole body by providing a simple animation from an exterior point of view. Equally importantly, it is currently freely available. To illustrate the opportunities of e-learning, consider, for example, the iliopsoas muscle group (Fig. 6) and its function in hip flexion. This muscle

Fig. 6: Iliopsoas muscle group

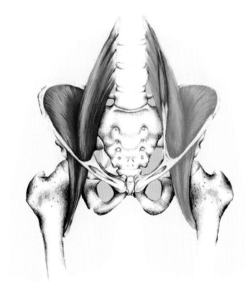

Fig. 6: Illustration by Aimee Jewitt-Harris ©

Fig. 7: Terminology matching task

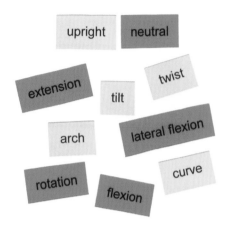

group sits deep within the body and students often find it difficult to imagine where it is and how it works. While popular imagery such as "lift the leg from underneath" might help dancers lengthen the leg in extensions *devant*, it can easily lead to anatomical confusion in students. The use of a short muscle animation clip alongside an image (Fig. 6) can, in contrast, help them understand more clearly how the iliopsoas generates hip flexion.

Repertoire

As many dance curricula require the study of repertoire, it seems apt to use this as a vehicle to better anatomical understanding. The study of Merce Cunningham repertoire, for example, can easily be linked to the study of the spine and its various movement directions. The following task can be given to students as early as their first encounter with Cunningham's work or adapted for different stages within their learning. Students are asked to view an extract of repertoire and complete the following tasks:

1. Identify and record the five different positions of the back and record them in diagrammatic form
2. Match the anatomical terminology with the technical names (Fig. 7)
3. Create a short movement motif that:
   Must use each position of the back at least once
   Should use arm/leg movements from the repertoire extract
   Could involve travelling
   Challenge include changes of level and direction

Students could also learn actual repertoire and then use chance procedures to alter the positions of the back or other anatomical aspects of the movement. Any other dance repertoire can be used to effectively explore anatomical principles in practice and the possibilities are almost endless.

Somatic practice

To illustrate how somatic practices can be used to provide a kinaesthetic experience of dance anatomy, consider the following two exercises related to turnout. The first (Fig. 8) is designed to provide students with a tactile sensation of correct leg alignment in turnout. Therabands are knotted in a loop at one end, placed around the instep of each foot and then wrapped around the legs twice. The dancer holds the loose end of each theraband and is ready to explore a variety of dance movements, including: *pliés, battements tendus, battements fondus, développés, grands battements,* etc. to feel the spiralling sensation of correctly facilitated turn out along the legs. Therabands can be purchased from most sports and fitness retailers and are available as single bands or on rolls of 20–50 metres.

The second exercise (Fig. 9) serves as a strengthening exercise for the turnout muscles. The dancer lies on their side with the knees bent and shoulders, hips and ankles aligned either in the middle of the room or, for less experienced dancers, against a wall. The core is engaged and the dancer externally rotates the top leg as far as they can before the pelvis begins to move. This exercise can be done with or without a theraband or the addition of the leg extension after each opening of the knees. The strength of the theraband

Fig 8: Turnaround proprioception exercise with therabands wrapped around the legs and feet.

and the number of repetitions can be varied in accordance with individual needs and experience.

Both activities are easily embedded in or revisited during a technique class with a focus on turnout. The kinaesthetic understanding gained from such somatic exercises can help students immensely to enhance and self- or peer-assess dance technique. Of course, somatic work can also address any other anatomical

Fig 9: Turnout strengthening exercise with theraband tied around the knees (this can also be done without theraband or an added leg extension).

Fig. 8 & 9: Photographs by Janine Streuli; Dancer: Mary Green

concepts or structures, such as posture, core stability, breathing, flexibility, strength and the use of the feet, among many other topics, and it is incredibly valuable to establish an embodied understanding of dance anatomy.

Choreography

Finally, anatomical principles can be used as a stimulus for choreography. The Cunningham-based repertoire task already contained a choreography element but combined it with the study of repertoire. The task-sheet below (Fig. 10) shows a simple resource that serves as a starting point for creative work that requires students to collaborate to apply their understanding of the structure and function of different types of joints.

Body Part	Movement Direction
example: right elbow	example: flexion
example: left hip	example: external rotation

- **Student 1** completes the body part column (identifying a given number of different joints)
- **Student 2** completes the movement direction column (thinking critically about what actions are possible at each given joint to select one)
- **Student 3** creates a motif based on the joint actions prescribed

Apart from applying and revising anatomical knowledge and thus developing a more detailed understanding of how the body works, this task can also help students create more imaginative movement material for choreography.

Conclusion

I would like to share the thoughts of some AS students who have experienced this teaching model in practice:

The multi-method approach is:

"good because it ticks everyone's fancy" and it "helps make your knowledge more applicable in different scenarios".

PBL "helps your thinking skills in the sense that you are able to question yourself more".

"we are learning independently and are trying to work things out for ourselves, this means that we are actually working."

Learning anatomy "gives you a better under-standing of what you are doing to your body. I think it really helps you so that you do not do any damage to any of your muscles or joints".

"Even if you don't go on to do dance as a career, you know how to prevent injuries."

Clearly, high quality dance anatomy instruction can not only educate dancers about using their bodies effectively and safely but it can also contribute to our students' lifelong wellbeing beyond dance.

References

3D4Medical. *Muscle System Pro III*. Computer Software. *Apple App Store*. Vers. 3.3. 3D4 Medical, October 2012. Web. 20 April 2014. https://itunes.apple.com/us/app/muscle-system-pro-ii-nova/id364596328?mt=8

AQA *GCE AS and A Level Specification Dance*. 2013. Web. 20 April 2014. http://filestore.aqa.org.uk/subjects/specifications/alevel/AQA-2230-W-SP-14.PDF

Agur, Anne M. R. and Arthur F. Dalley. *Grant's Atlas of Anatomy*. Twelfth Edition. Philadelphia: Wolters Kluwer Health/Lippincott Williams & Wilkins, 2009. Print.

Anyaehie, Ugochukwu, S. et al. "Comparative Evaluation of Active Learning and the Traditional Lectures in Physiology: a Case Study of 200 Level Medical Laboratory Students of Imo State University, Owerri". *Nigerian Journal of Physiological Sciences: Official Publication of the Physiological Society of Nigeria* 22:1-2 (2007): 117-121. Print.

Becker, S., et al. 2003 "Integration of Study Material in the Problem Based Learning Method". *Curationis* 26:1 (2003): 56-61. Print.

Brinson, Peter and Fiona Dick. *Fit to Dance?* London: Dance UK, 1996. Print.

Daniels, Kathryn. "Teaching Anatomically-Sound Turn-out". *Journal of Dance Education* 7:3 (2007): 91-94. Print.

Davis, Margery, H. and Ronald, M. Harden. "AMEE Medical Education Guide No. 15: Problem-based Learning: a Practical Guide". *Medical Teacher* 21:2 (1999): 130-140. Print.

Drake, Richard, L. "A Unique, Innovative, and Clinically Oriented Approach to Anatomy Education". *Academic Medicine: Journal of the Association of American Medical Colleges* 82:5 (2007): 475-478. Print.

El Moamly, Amal, A. "Problem-Based Learning Benefits for Basic Sciences Education". *Anatomical Sciences Education* 1 (2008): 189-190. Print.

General Medical Council (GMC). *Tomorrow's Doctors*. 1993. Web. 20 April 2014. www.gmc-uk.org/Tomorrows_Doctors_1993.pdf_25397206.pdf

Hillman, Susan, K. *Interactive Functional Anatomy*. Second Edition. London: Primal Pictures Ltd., 2009. DVD ROM.

Laws, Helen. *Fit to Dance 2*. London: Dance UK, 2005. Print.

Pengelly, Fritha. "Anatomy for Dance: An Expanded Design. *Journal of Dance Education* 11:1 (2010): 77-82. Print.

Percac, Sanja, and Daniel A. Goodenough. "Problem Based Teaching and Learning as a Bridge from Basic Anatomy to Clinical Clerkships". *Surgical and Radiologic Anatomy*. Web. 20:3 (1998): 203-207. www.authormapper.com/search.aspx?val=keyword%3AMedica PDF file.

Rizzolo, Lawrence J., et al. 2010 "Design, Implementation, and Evaluation of an Innovative

Anatomy Course". *Anatomical Sciences Education*. Web. (2010): 1-12. www.*onlinelibrary.wiley.com/doi/10.1002/ase.152/abstract* PDF file.

Salk, Jennifer. 2005 "Teaching Modern Technique through Experiential Anatomy". *Journal of Dance Education* 5:3 (2005): 97-102. Print.

Sheffield, Scott. *GetBodySmart: An Online Textbook about Human Anatomy and Physiology*. 2001-2014. Web. 10 April 2014. www.getbodysmart.com/index.htm

Vogel, Deborah. "Teaching Anatomy". *Dance Teacher* 29:3 (2007): 50-53. Print.

Xu, Bo. "Traditional Anatomy Teaching and Problem-based-learning is there a Middle Way?" *ANZ Journal of Surgery* 78:1-2 (2008): 6. Print.

Yiou, René and Daniel Goodenough. "Applying Problem-based learning to the Teaching of Anatomy: the Example of Harvard Medical School". *Surgical and Radiologic Anatomy: SRA* 28:2 (2006): 189-194. Print.

Acknowledgements

The author would like to thank Josephine Bell and Gillian Lenton for agreeing to be interviewed during the research phase of this project. Both contributed very valuable insights and ideas that are gratefully acknowledged.

Thank you also to all the students who participated in the research and willingly shared their thoughts.

JANINE STREULI

Janine is Head of Learning and Teaching at the Faculty of Education of the Royal Academy of Dance. She has been a full-time academic at the RAD since 2010 and tutors across a range of undergraduate, postgraduate and professional programmes. She has managed both the BA (Hons) Ballet Education as well as the Postgraduate Certificate in Education: Dance Teaching, and in January 2014 she took on the role of Head of Learning and Teaching.

Prior to joining the RAD, Janine had an extensive freelance career, teaching dance in the private and public sectors. During that time, she also taught Yoga and Pilates in numerous contexts. Janine is trained in ballet and contemporary dance and her research interests cover health, safe practice and innovative pedagogy. Alongside her work for the Faculty of Education, Janine continues to tutor on the Dance A-Level for the RAD Dance School and also teaches ballet for a South London dance school.

Holistic Ballet: Dancing from the Inside Out

BY CLARE GUSS-WEST

Today, ballet students and professionals regularly turn to alternative training methods such as yoga, Pilates and weight training to supplement their daily ballet class. They find it insufficient as a standalone training to meet the demands of today's choreographers and diverse repertoire. Yet classical ballet is an essentially 'organic' and complete training system, and a discernable evolution is taking place. Professionals and teachers are reaching beyond dance to study other related movement practices, distilling and bringing the most effective elements back to dance practice and to the renewal of ballet.

Supported by the latest findings in sports research and neuroscience, *'holistic ballet'*[1] was developed in this spirit, incorporating essential elements from non-western somatic movement practice, notably Chi Kung (Qi Gong). Scientific research and Chi Kung practice are translated into accessible practical tools for teachers that can be directly integrated into traditional exercises to maximise effectiveness, facilitate learning and enhance performance.

The term *holistic*, meaning whole or multi-dimensional, is commonly applied to the field of complementary health where the essence is to address the whole person, rather than a series of isolated symptoms. In ballet terms it similarly implies addressing the whole dancer, teaching a balanced understanding of the inner and the outer dimensions – physical, mental, emotional and spiritual – that contribute to the delivery of quality artistic movement.

In traditional ballet training there is a common assumption that more effort will lead to improvement and mastery. We are typically taught to 'hold more, turnout more, pull up more' rather than to be attentive and let the movement flow. In sports science and somatic practices however, it is known that more effort leads to more of the same result or, worse, to movement dysfunction and diminished results. As a long-term training approach, this paves the way for chronic fatigue and potential injury.

With its 'less is more' approach, *'holistic ballet'* provides an alternative tool for the dancer, applying the focused intention of the

[1] Guss-West, Clare. Integrated approach to ballet training, termed 'holistic ballet'™ was developed in Paris 2010 in pilot teaching and research studies and was officially presented at Tamed (German Dance Medicine Association) 2010, and IADMS (International Association of Dance Medicine and Science) 2011, and taught on several RAD Faculty of Education programmes.

Opposite: Clare Guss-West by Finnish National photographer Aku Suikosaari.

Abovee: Clare with students of
Balletschule Lambert, Switzerland.

mind to provide strength, rather than effort,
to control. The holistic approach respects the
body, understanding it to be an intelligent,
self-regulating sensory organism. Far from
being 'lazy', as some of us have learnt, the body
makes millions of decisions every second for
our maximum efficiency and wellbeing without
our conscious intervention. Our role becomes
one of listening, responding and dancing 'with'
our body, rather than attempting to control
or push against its nature.

When asked to produce an action representing
extreme effort, dancers will almost without
exception, produce a static, contracted pose,
withholding breath, and then collapse as they

run out of oxygen and energy (and then
laugh in recognition at how unsustainable
that movement was). Yet this all too often
remains the concept of effort they hold in
their minds and with which they approach
challenging dance movements. Contracted
movements, as I have argued elsewhere,
"are rigid and incapable of responding to
any eventuality. Constricted energy is
soon exhausted." (West)

Comparing the effectiveness of this image
of effort with the 'less is more' approach
produces a silence as many dancers experience
for the first time without effort, a "powerful
movement with constant, stable energy."[2]

The ancient practice of Chi Kung, or *Energy Work*, focuses primarily on the inner work of the moving body through mastery of energy, breathing techniques to replenish energy and systematic use of the mind to facilitate effortless extension, line, speed and precision. It respects the interconnectedness of body, mind and spirit with three foundational focuses: posture and alignment, breathing and energy, and intention and awareness, and is the basis of the related forms T'ai Chi and Kung Fu. The form shares so many principles with classical ballet that one might imagine that the Royal Dancing Masters of Louis XIV, at the height of the Franco-Chinese commercial and cultural exchange, were familiar with the popular Eastern movement form, making it an ideal complementary somatic technique.

In traditional ballet training, the use of the breath is seldom addressed systematically. Dancers typically hold the breath during the most strenuous or demanding movements, producing diminished results and a lack of power and stamina. When breath *is* addressed in traditional training, the focus is typically on the 'in-breath' and yet this conscious action engages the muscles of the shoulders, chest and neck increasing upper body tension. The 'in-breath' is a natural reflex action and it is in fact the 'out-breath', the complete and efficient emptying of the lungs, that does not occur naturally. In *'holistic ballet'* conscious breathing

is choreographed and coordinated to be 'one' with the nature and demands of individual movements or phrases, whether explosive, sustained or transition movements, to maximise energy and speed of response. During the 'in-breath' we gather oxygen as 'potential' in the lungs by making space and allowing breath to fill the body cavity. The moment of the 'out-breath' *is* the moment of power and replenishment, creating an explosive movement of oxygen and energy to our extremities to power our billions of cells and nerve-endings. Experiencing the power of this fundamental focus, dancers find a simple but effective tool to tackle any arduous *adage* that produces immediate visible results.

The Chinese symbols for breath and for energy are the same, implying that effective breathing literally is the key to our vital energy source. Without the mastery of the breath, there will not be a successful renewing of energy. Coincident with the continuum of oxygen surrounding us, is a continuous field of energy, the electromagnetic or Universal Energy Field. Energy, as it gathers around and travels through the human body, can be directed and channeled for maximum effect. Energy is thus not personal to the individual but is drawn from the Universal Energy Field. Our role as a dancer is to learn how to continuously replenish this energy with the support of the breathing action. An illustrative Chinese proverb would be "we should first fill the teapot before pouring the tea".

The renewal of energy can be consciously facilitated via various key areas of the body:

[2] Cannes Dance Festival – *'holistic ballet'*™ workshop feedback from a student of l'Ecole Superieure de Danse, Palais de Congress, Cannes. Nov 2013.

through the elongation of the spine and neutral pelvis, particularly at the points of the occipital skull and sacrum. A simple Chi Kung exercise consciously circulates energy upwards from the sacrum, through the elongated spine and occipital skull and allows it to descend, releasing the front of the body in a continuous circle. This simple exercise promotes the ideal classical posture and alignment. In *'holistic ballet'* we seek the natural 'neutral' moments, transition movements such as *fondu, demi-plié, envelopé* through *retiré, temps liés* and transfer of weight to create space in the body, expanding rather than contracting to allow unobstructed energy uptake and flow.

"The whole is greater than the sum of its individual parts," Aristotle declared and nowhere is that more true than in quality artistic dance performance. The pressure on dancers to achieve outstanding technique is fierce and it is understandable that training might become unbalanced to focus on external results of individual body parts such as the height of the leg, the curve of the back or the angle of the *pointe*, but this focus on an individual part comes at the expense of the whole and often at the expense of artistry.

When we imagine the body as a series of individual parts, this is exactly the result we achieve – a series of movements of limbs that are not integrated into a vision of the whole, into the dance. From a Chi Kung perspective, focusing on an individual body part or part action produces movement dysfunction and energy inefficiency. Chi Kung teaches that "where the mind will go, energy and blood will follow", so to project the mind into just one leg, for example, will inevitably mean sacrificing the strength of other core components such as stability, balance and fluidity.

Awareness, conscious intention and imagination are key tools in an holistic approach. We move beyond the imbalance of isolated corrections to visualise movement as a multi-dimensional whole. The mind is such an effective programmer of our movement that sports trainers today make frequent use of static, closed-eye imaging of an optimum movement sequence prior to any physical realisation for maximum efficiency. This practice takes only a few seconds and can easily be added to supplement the traditional 'marking' of exercises or *enchaînements* prior to physical execution.

In order to achieve a stable, expressive *arabesque* for example, we visualise the impact of the whole movement intention and project our energy out through the entire body and beyond like a *'shooting star'* simultaneously in five directions. This foundational action is established in an initial proprioceptive exercise with fellow students to create awareness of the simultaneous directions. The multi-dimensional, proprioceptive sensation can be easily recalled by the dancer in the future to reproduce the desired intention. In *adage* and *grand allegro* we trace in our 'mind's eye' the gyroscopic relationship of arcs, curves and lines of energy as we project them out in space – balancing both the inner awareness and a distant outward focus and vision. Through

Opposite RESEO/Finnish National Ballet 2014. Photographer: Aku Suikosaari.

peer observation exercises we establish that "as we project our intention and energy, so is it perceived by the observer", developing the student's ability to 'see' beyond the physical body, to coach and to master the 'inner' work of dance.

The effectiveness of this projection of intention and focus from the inside-out beyond the body is confirmed by sports movement researcher Dr Gabriele Wulf to enhance kinesthetic learning, mastery and performance (2013), such that beginner swimmers demonstrate the same effortless grace as experienced swimmers when imagining and focusing on the movement of the surrounding water (Wulf and Shea). Significant benefits are found from projecting intention beyond the individual body actions in terms of balance, consistency, accuracy, energy and effort. The minimum muscular effort that ensues from this distant focus means that speed is optimised and stamina and endurance are increased. The research further concurs with *'holistic ballet'* and Chi Kung practice – that the more distant the image and focus beyond the physical body, the more effective it is in promoting effortless, masterful movement. This technique produces not only an immediate effect on performance and learning, but also a permanent effect in retention and capabilities.

Focusing intention out beyond the physical body encourages an optimum mind state referred to in Chi Kung as 'No Mind' – not a vacant, unthinking mind but an alert state of total attentiveness, free from thought or dialogue. The 'No Mind' state parallels what neuroscience terms the Alpha brain wave state associated with masterful, professional performance (Adee), resulting in a relaxed body operating on automatic with reduced pulse, blood pressure and breathing, and suppressed thought. This state can be cultivated in ballet teaching but necessitates a heightened awareness of the role of the ballet teacher as learning facilitator. Of primary importance is the conscious choice of teaching vocabulary and an understanding of the power of words to 'enable' or 'disable'. Secondly, it requires the systematic implementation of inspirational distant images and focus, consciously selected to facilitate enhanced learning. This Alpha brain state is particularly effective for more complex motor actions such as *Pirouettes*. As many professional dancers discover intuitively, by removing the cognitive dialogue and the focus on control of the action of individual parts, we allow the body in its own wisdom to find the optimum solution to the movement challenge.

Wulf's findings provide food for thought for the ballet teacher. They reveal that movement efficiency and learning deteriorate significantly in both professionals and beginners, if performers are asked to direct their focus to the action of individual body parts. In the movement practices analysed, teaching focus and feedback was predominantly physical body-part specific (70–95.5%). Body-part focus is shown to trigger a 'choking' (Wulf 2007) or freezing reaction that spreads from the individual part through an entire muscle chain to produce a global movement dysfunction. A consideration for holistic ballet teachers would be the balance therefore between body-part feedback, shown to be effective if restricted to a minimum, and the alternative use of a distant intention, image and focus, shown to be more effective the more it is implemented.

Scientists now turn to another potential factor of effective training: the role of enjoyment and joy in mediating learning. During the *'holistic ballet'* research, the professional dancers reported a renewed enjoyment in ballet training as one of the unexpected benefits. Even before the scientific analysis is complete, as teaching artists we instinctively understand the interconnectedness of ballet on all levels – physical, mental, emotional and spiritual. We move beyond technique in this complete, 'organic' form to redress the training focus on to the essential inner dimensions of dance. Harnessing the power of the mind and the intelligence to support the physical demands, we focus on the emotion, the musicality and the joy of dance as keys to enhance learning and promote quality artistic performance.

References

Adee, Sally. "Zap your brain into the zone: Fast track to pure focus". *New Scientist.* Web. 06 February 2012. www.newscientist.com/article/mg21328501.600-zap-your-brain-into-the-zone-fast-track-to-pure-focus.html

West, Clare. *The Energy Source.* London: Prion Books, 1997. Print.

Wulf, Gabriele and Charles Shea. "Enhancing motor learning through external-focus instructions and feedback". *Human Movement Science* 18.4 (1999): 553–571. Print.

Wulf, Gabriele. *Attention and Motor Skill Learning.* Champaign: Human Kinetics, 2007. Print.

– – –. "Attentional focus and motor learning: A review of 15 years". *International Review of Sport and Exercise Psychology* 6 (2013): 77–104.

CLARE GUSS-WEST

Clare is a classical and contemporary dance teacher, choreographer, musician, holistic health practitioner and author. She created 'holistic ballet'™ approach to training for teachers and 'dancing longevity'® – 'Dance practice for older learners' for the RAD, (PDPTC, CPD, BABE) and for L'Ecole Superieure de Danse Rosella Hightower, Cannes. She delivers introductory workshops in both subjects for the International Association of Dance Medicine & Science, School of the Arts, Singapore; Nanyang Academy of Fine Arts, Singapore; Cornish College for the Arts, Seattle; and Pro Arte, Vancouver.

Clare is dance moderator and committee member of RESEO: The European Network for Opera & Dance Education, representing and promoting creative learning in over 80 major opera and ballet companies throughout Europe.

Breaking Down Barriers: Magpie Dance

BY AVRIL HITMAN

In the UK, adults with learning disabilities face staggering health inequalities and poor wellbeing. The challenges they face are complex and numerous, indicated in the social determinants of health such as genetic factors, issues with communication, poor diet, and insufficient exercise (Health Inequalities). For nearly 30 years, Magpie Dance has supported people of all ages to overcome such barriers to wellbeing through an inclusive approach to dance.

Magpie Dance was founded by offering weekly 45 minute recreational dance sessions for adults with learning disabilities in a social service centre. Our programmes have since developed to encompass inclusive dance for disabled people with a range of abilities and learning needs. We became a registered charity and Company Ltd by Guarantee in 1993, and were accredited by the Council for Dance Education and Training (CDET).

Magpie strives to unlock individual potential and ability, and to be at the forefront of dance for people with learning disabilities. We aim to achieve this vision through targeted outcomes:

- improve non-verbal communication with people with learning disabilities and their support workers;
- enable progression and ambitious skill development in dance for people with learning disabilities;
- enable co-operation to improve confidence, and
- empower through skill development.

Our sustained dance sessions give particular attention to improving difficulties in communication. In doing so, they attend to the limited verbal abilities of the participants, and the fact that support workers are often unaware of how non-verbal and other approaches can improve their interaction with people with learning disabilities. As one Magpie participant noted:

> "Magpie has had a beneficial effect on every aspect of my life by increasing my confidence, improving my communication skills, helping me to be more aware of others and to work as a team. Taking part in performances has been a great boost to my confidence and a source of self-belief, self-esteem, teamwork, excitement and fun. The physical aspect has also helped my balance, agility and general fitness."

Opposite: Photo credit Gigi Giannella.

Our work hinges on three strands: participation, performance and training.

Participation programmes:

Open and tailored classes in the community:
• More than 200 adults and young people with learning disabilities access our sessions through more than 200 dance classes every year in South East London. These longstanding programmes offer twice-weekly sessions for ages 11 to 25, as well as for adults and their support workers. We also run a weekly session for adults who choreograph and perform their own work.
• For many participants, attending our sessions is the only physical activity they take part in during their week.

Dance in healthcare environments:
• In partnership with the Oxleas NHS Foundation Trust since 2012, we have been providing bespoke sessions for clients in day service and in-patient treatment centres. Clients have a range of learning disabilities, including autism and associated conditions such as dementia.
• The Oxleas classes enable clients to take part in regular healthy activity, improve their communications with their peers and with staff, and, ultimately, to enhance their independence. Integral to this programme are training sessions, which help both staff and their clients to learn to interact in new ways.
• The Lottery Reaching Communities fund has supported this work for over four years and, in the first year, was evaluated by the Oxleas

Psychology Department. They used the system of 'care mapping' to explore the impact on the participants in terms of personal development (confidence, self-esteem and communication), improved wellbeing and increased participation.

The evaluation reported that of those who attended:
• 67% demonstrated improvement in confidence (as observed by staff and through independent mapping observation and interview);
• 73% showed improvement in self-esteem in general;
• 67% showed improvements in the group setting;
• 53% showed improvements in non-verbal communication skills in general; and
• 67% showed improvements when working as a group.

Staff also reported an improvement in wellbeing for participants with autism and more challenging needs. They were observed to be very actively joining in for over two thirds of the time in the sessions – an impressive figure considering the nature of their disabilities and low levels of participation in other structured activities.

> "It was very good to see the positive effects the classes visibly had on the participants, and the flexible structure of the sessions which also gave people the ability to have influence over the sessions and to make their own choices."
> Peter Wanless, Chief Executive, Big Lottery Fund on a visit to a Magpie class

Photo credit Rachel Cherry.

Performance programmes:

In collaboration with established companies, we encourage and support participants to develop performance pieces to a professional standard. We have worked with Siobhan Davies Dance, and were also funded by the Arts Council England to collaborate with New Adventures artists on a new piece based on *Edward Scissorhands*. 'The Ed Effect' explored exclusion, being different and trying to fit within a diverse community. Public performances have taken place at venues such as Trinity Laban, Peacock Theatre, O2, Churchill Theatre, the South Bank Centre, Trafalgar Square and the Albany Deptford.

Our presence in the public arena offers an important means of breaking down barriers by challenging assumptions and preconceptions regarding learning disabled dancers. We also open up routes for young disabled people in dance across South East London as a consortium partner with Trinity Laban, Candoco Dance Company and Greenwich Dance.

"It was excellent, fantastic, amazing and extraordinary; I don't think you can get better than that. I was amazed at how professional our dancers were and how brilliant their timing was." Magpie dancer parent at Co Motion performance, Trinity Laban

We have also embarked on an ambitious 'High Fliers' programme for talented dancers with learning disabilities who would like to take their skills further and become part of a professional dance company. To this end, we commissioned a viability study to examine training pathways and progression routes to help them.

The study found that there are very limited opportunities for training of this nature, and highlighted the fact that there only a few paid dancers with learning disabilities in the profession. Given our considerable experience of working in the sector, we believe that we can make a difference to this state of affairs by challenging the industry to recognise other working models. The cultural landscape needs to better reflect the nature of society by recognising that dancers with learning disabilities have a vital role to play. Through investment from Esmée Fairbairn Foundation, this new artistic programme begins in September 2014 for gifted and talented dancers with learning disabilities. The ambition of 'High Fliers' is to change attitudes, make more choices available, and therein to give more equal and consistent opportunities for learning disabled dancers to progress their skills further.

"…it was incredibly inspiring to see dancers of different abilities really rise to meet the opportunity of working with a leading professional dance company. It was wonderful to see a collaboration of this kind as part of the Big Dance programme." Anne Hartley, Arts Council England (Summer 2012) on the Magpie 'Big Dance' performance

Training programmes:

Continuing Professional Development in the dance, education, and health sectors: Magpie's community programmes include a dedicated Peer Mentoring scheme, in which participants take on responsible roles within the sessions. We also have a wealth of experience delivering Continued Professional Development workshops in special and mainstream schools for primary and secondary school teachers as well as for dance practitioners and professionals. We have delivered training in inclusive dance for clients including Trinity Laban, Greenwich Dance, the Royal Academy of Dance, Dance Resource Belfast, New Adventures dance artists, Youth Dance England, The Metropolitan Police (Disability Hate Crime) and the NHS.

Our work in the health sector focused on training for NHS nurses working with clients with learning disabilities in order to improve the quality of the care and experience from both sides. Improved non-verbal communications were highlighted as an important aspect of enhancing wellbeing, and the feedback was very positive:

"I learned confidence and strategies and ideas for supporting students that are difficult to engage"

"Achievable! Motivating, enthusiastic to try ideas, hundreds of ideas to take to the classroom. Confidence boosting day!"

"Thoroughly enjoyed the experience, hands on, creative, allowed independent development … Excellent … My mind is overflowing with new ideas! I think I will have a new approach and not be so stuck and rigid … fresh inspiration … lovely session … great workshop – well-presented and lots of fun"
Participants from Magpie INSET training days.

Further education partnerships:
We are currently piloting a new training programme in partnership with Canterbury Christ Church University, in which we will deliver an inclusive dance module for second and third-year students as part of their degree course. The students will gain 'hands on' experience with pupils (primary and secondary) from a local special school.

The broader impact of our work:
In a recent survey we asked our participants and carers in *what ways they thought their life had changed* because of attending Magpie Dance.
• 83% said we had improved their confidence
• 81% said we had improved their life and learning skills
• 80% feel we have improved their health

• 80% said we made them feel better about themselves
• 72% have improved the ways they communicate with others

Our work and its impact go beyond basic care. At Magpie Dance we believe wholeheartedly that disability is not a barrier to progression. And, with wider opportunities for participation, increased chances for people with learning disabilities to perform and wider availability of training to support this, everyone can be helped to unlock their potential.

Reference
Health Inequalities & People with Learning Disabilities in the UK, Web 2010. http://www. improvinghealthandlives.org.uk/uploads/doc/ vid_7479_IHaL2010–3HealthInequality2010.pdf

AVRIL HITMAN
After graduating from the London College of Dance and Drama in 1975, Avril taught dance in mainstream settings for ten years, after which she began to use dance in working with people with learning disabilities. Her work has also included three visits to Bangladesh, supported by the British Council, leading creative dance workshops for young people with learning disabilities and their teachers.

In 1985 she founded and is the current Artistic Director of Magpie Dance Company, which delivers over 200 sessions for over 200 people (aged 11 through to adults) annually through its participation, performance and training programmes. 2014 marks the 30th anniversary of Magpie Dance, as well as the launch of High Fliers, a company class for gifted and talented learning disabled dancers.

Avril has delivered dance workshops in Sweden for an international Theatre Festival, is a core member of the National Inclusive Dance Network as well as a Fellow of the Royal Society of Arts.

The Adult Ballet Learner: A Personal Reflection

BY ROSIE GERHARD

In recent years and months, dance schools and institutions, local newspapers, national magazines and online news services have been reporting a burgeoning enthusiasm for ballet amongst adults ("Ballet: the new fitness trend"; Ellison; Plymouth Dance Agency; Robinson; Royal Academy of Dance). However, I myself have noticed numbers growing substantially since the late 1980s when I began attending classes at London's Pineapple Studios, The Royal Opera House and Dance Attic. From the familiar faces that I see, it seems that many people, like me, attend on a regular basis and continue dancing over decades. While some begin dancing as adults, others return to ballet having studied it as children and teenagers, and a small number of former professional dancers attend for pleasure.

Currently I attend two or three classes a week (including a private lesson), taught by two different teachers: Jo Bell, with whom I have studied for over twenty years, and Olga Semenova, whose classes I have attended for approximately fifteen years. Most of my fellow dancers are female, the youngest in their 20s and the eldest in their 70s.

Opposing views on adult ballet

My thoughts about the differing perceptions of adult ballet were set off by two *Dancing Times* articles (2006 and 2012) which looked at the achievements an amateur adult ballet dancer might hope to attain. Diane Coyle was attending up to five classes a week:

> 'Anybody who is not completely delusional will realise they will not look like a ballet dancer. They will probably not be very good at it. But that isn't the point. The struggle to achieve beauty is what matters. There is a powerful sense of validation and self-worth from, say, doing a beautiful *port-de-bras* even if you will never get your leg above 45 degrees." (cited in McCarthy 27).

In stark contrast, Frederick Lewis, who started ballet at the age of 45, clearly believes that not only can an adult beginner be "very good at it", but she can even be trained to professional standards:

> "Is it ridiculous for a woman in her forties to dream of becoming a ballerina? … [It] is entirely possible that in our lifetime a ballerina will emerge in maturity …

Opposite: Photo credit David Tett.

"[E]xperts … concur that an adult beginner could never attain the level of fitness demanded by the rigours of ballet technique. This is nonsense … For a determined individual the difficult process of slowly building up suppleness, strength and stamina is probably part of the attraction." (35–36)

Clearly, even though both of these women are learning ballet as adult beginners, their understanding of the relationship between ballet and the mature body seems to be diametrically opposed.

I took ballet classes once a week from the age of about seven to fourteen. When I returned to ballet in my late twenties, I remember my body feeling completely different. I sensed for the first time a battle going on between ballet and my body. Yet neither of the experiences of Diane Coyle or Frederick Lewis resembles my own – I can safely say that I can lift my leg above 45 degrees, but that I will never be a ballerina. I am, furthermore, familiar with a number of middle-aged women about whom I could make exactly the same statement.

Ballet and the young

With its emphasis on early professional training leading to a performing career of perhaps two decades (Turner and Wainwright), its proclivity for a prepubescent body type, and a focus on youthful characters, ballet as an art form does tend to be visibly associated with youth. Perhaps this in part accounts for the susceptibility of adult ballet learners (and this clearly includes Diane Coyle) to the notion of

the body's "inevitable decline" (Schwaiger xi) and the narrative of enfeeblement associated with the ageing process (Tulle 4–6). And, in the studio, changing room and around the post-class coffee table, disappointments are voiced. These are mainly by those who continued with lessons well into their teens, interrupted their studies for number of years, and now deem it an impossibility to reach the same level of attainment that they achieved in their youth. Typical complaints are: "Of course I can't dance like I used to" and "My *arabesque* line's gone".

It is clear that the ageing process does take its toll on the body, and will therefore have an impact on a person's ballet technique: muscle wasting and weakening, wear and tear on the joints and supporting structures, stiffening in the joints, and depleted bone mineral density cannot be ignored. However, many of the factors with which I have struggled in ballet lessons over the years (and surely I am not alone in this) are a result of my particular muscular-skeletal make-up, rather than a consequence of the ageing process.

A virtuous circle

One of the primary fundaments of ballet technique is, of course, turn-out. However, I have little turn-out in the hips due to the configuration of my joints, and what I have is difficult to capitalise on due to tightness in the ligaments of the hips and hip flexors. While ballet assumes physical symmetry, there is a substantial discrepancy in my leg length, noticeable a-symmetry in my neck and shoulders, and even my minimal turn-out

Opposite: Photo credit Eric Richmond.

is uneven. In addition to these imbalances (and possibly exacerbated by them), life circumstances and accident have caused me to suffer from a bulging disc in my spine, and an osteoarthritic right knee.

The result of these physical drawbacks is that I have been unable to do a *grand plié* for over ten years and have hardly jumped for several years; neither have I ever been able to execute high extensions. Nevertheless, in the need to deal with these same drawbacks, I have found ways to engage in ballet that give both myself and my teachers the impression that I am still developing my physical knowledge and understanding of ballet, thereby becoming a 'better' dancer over the years.

Osteoarthritis in the knee and acute back pain impact not only on dance classes but on movement essential to everyday life, including walking, climbing stairs, sitting, lifting and carrying. Therefore I have been forced to pay attention to my body and have been doing physiotherapy exercises for over ten years, and more recently Pilates too. Additionally, and without fail, I do a warm up and cool down before and after every ballet class. This has given me advantages in that much of my daily pain has receded, and that I began to develop my kinaesthetic sense: I become much more knowledgeable about my body and the way in which it moves; a knowledge which I have applied to my ballet classes.

Through the necessity of targeting specific muscles in physiotherapy and Pilates, I have become kinaesthetically aware of individual muscles. As a result, in my ballet classes the alignment of my body can be felt, rather than simply checked in a mirror. And once, with the help of my teachers, the correct alignment can be kinaesthetically perceived, the process of gaining control over the muscles can begin: I start to make appropriate adjustments and to strengthen the relevant muscles in order to hold the alignment. This process has become a virtuous circle for me.

As an example of the progress I have made in ballet, the following exchange recently took place between my teacher Jo Bell and myself:

"Today I was pretty dissatisfied with myself – my body felt so sluggish, and everything felt like such an effort. However, as I was frustratedly musing over this in the shower, I realised that 15 years ago when my body felt like it was working poorly it meant something completely different: when I turned to the 2nd side at the barre, I regularly felt that I had a completely different body to the 1st side, like I was a jigsaw puzzle that someone had put together all wrongly. I would feel no control over what I was doing at all. So today, even though it didn't seem like I was a achieving much, I realise the fact that I could *feel* my 4th position pirouette prep was too wide after you'd corrected me, rather than just be told again or see it in the mirror, is actually really empowering. It's the first step to progress.

My current body feels far more cohesive, harmonious and in control than my body of 15 years ago. Even when it's feeling uncooperative and inflexible."

Opposite: Photo credit Eric Richmond.

My teacher replied:

"I agree. If only we had some comparative film footage I think you would be amazed! Even in the last year there have been extraordinary changes, particularly in your 'core'. It's great that you recognise that."

Cohesion, harmony and control

The sense of cohesion, harmony and control derives not only from the process of 'internal' observation that I have described, but also through highly developed 'external' observation skills that I acquired during my study of Labanotation to advanced level. I use these skills constantly when observing my teachers and watching professional dancers. And from these observations I find new elements of ballet to work on, ones that I find far more fascinating than the contentious *grand plié*, high extensions, or even the jumps that I am currently seldom able to perform. Indeed, co-ordination, line and musicality – the three areas that I have been working on recently – all afford a sense of cohesion, harmony and control.

While co-ordination, line and musicality may not be considered the principle aspects of technique to be mastered, they emerged as essential components of ballet in the lecture and masterclass series, *A Focus on Style*, held at The Royal Ballet School. In the sessions on the English style, conducted by Anita Young from The Royal Ballet School, she highlighted all three of these features continuously and gave repeated corrections on them. Irina Sitnikova from the Vaganova Academy, conducting

equivalent sessions on the Russian style, repeatedly noted that her students were not co-ordinating their arms and legs, and urged them to do so, commenting that as a student she had habitually moved her arms too late to achieve full co-ordination with the rest of the body.

The corrections and comments made by these professional teachers may suggest that co-ordinating movements of the legs, arms, upper back and head is not as straightforward for a flexible professional ballet student as executing a high *arabesque* or *développé*. While such an extension would be impossible for me, primarily on account of my bony structure, this negates neither the importance nor the complexity of co-ordination suggested by the teaching of Anita Young and Irina Sitnikova, or indeed of my own teacher Olga Semenova, also trained at the Vaganova Ballet Academy.

A beautiful but complex *port-de-bras*

Co-ordination is perhaps most clearly discernible in *port de bras*; yet Diane Coyle's words seem rather dismissive of the *port de bras* in comparison to the ability of the dancer to raise her leg above 45 degrees. The choreographer Frederick Ashton, on the other hand, pays tribute to both the importance and complexity of mastering "a beautiful *port-de-bras*":

"If I had my way, I would always insist that all dancers should daily do the wonderful [Cecchetti] *ports de bras*, especially beginners. It inculcates a wonderful feeling for line and correct positioning and the use of head movement and épaulement, which, if correctly absorbed, will be of incalculable use throughout a dancer's career." (Cited in Glasstone 8)

Performing a *port de bras* is, I would argue, a far more sophisticated action than lifting the leg. It requires co-ordinated movements of the trunk, head and arms; as the arms lift, lower, open and close, simultaneously subtly rotating, lengthening and contracting, the hands and fingers engage in finely articulate movements. And, of course, it relies on strong core stability that allows the trunk the freedom to extend, flex and rotate.

The ballerina Gelsey Kirkland, for instance, not only clearly devoted much time, deliberation and effort to developing the *port de bras* in Aurora's Act III variation to meet the rigours of her own performance standards, but she evidently considered the process of such import that she devoted almost three pages to a detailed description of rehearsal for this one phrase in the variation (220–23). So to me, the ability to perform a "beautiful *port-de-bras*" is no mean feat.

Just as it is easy to oversimplify the complexity of a *port de bras*, it is similarly tempting to think of creating a 'good' line simply in terms of the facility to raise the leg in *attitude* or *arabesque* to at least 90 degrees, and significantly higher in *penché*. However, my own understanding of line in ballet is a line through the whole body, including legs and feet, arms and hands, torso, shoulder-line, head and neck. While this is a great deal to think about, it does mean that even though ballet is based on ideals of movement, line can be adapted to suit the individual body, and is not reliant solely on flexibility and turn-out in the hips. And because it not reliant on this alone, line is something that I can constantly work on and improve. When I achieve what my teachers consider a good *arabesque, attitude* or *attitude greque* line, through working hard at feeling my body and understanding the complexity of what I am trying to accomplish, I experience a real sense of achievement.

Something that is less challenging for me, but no less absorbing, is finding relationships between the movement and the music, and using this to phrase the movement and give it a particular shape. Syncopating, suspending, emphasising or de-emphasising particular aspects of the *enchaînement*, in relation to its shape and how I hear the music, its rhythm, dynamics, textures and melody, gives me a satisfying sense of individualising the movement.

All of these aspects of ballet that I am working on require a certain degree of strength, stability and accuracy in weight placement and transference, but once again there is plenty of opportunity to work on these fundamentals in every ballet class. Further, the general progress made through working on such elements can sometimes have surprising results, such as when I unexpectedly find myself doing multiple *fouettés*, triple *pirouettes* or a challenging combination of turns.

So, I fundamentally disagree with both Diane Coyle and Frederick Lewis. Having continuously watched ballet companies of international repute over the past four decades, I cannot conceive of the possibility of an adult beginner acquiring the specialised skill and stamina to perform the likes of *Swan Lake*, MacMillan's *Manon* or even Ashton's Natalia Petrovna in *A Month in the Country*. However, my expectations of my own potential in ballet class far exceed the mere ability to raise my leg to above 45 degrees.

Paying attention to the body as an adult ballet learner over time can result in discovery. If pursued, this results in development and the sense of the body and mind in constant dialogue with one another – rather than a sense of the body in inevitable decline – leading to a feeling of empowerment rather than enfeeblement. And this feeling of empowerment can filter through into other areas of life, thereby having a positive impact on general everyday wellbeing. Two things are crucial to this process, however: both the student and teacher's willingness to commit to it.

References

"Ballet: the new fitness trend". MSN Her UK. 2014. Web. 29 May 2014. http://style.uk.msn.com/health/ballet-the-new-fitness-trend#scpshrjmd

Ellison, Jo. "Raising the barre". *Vogue* June 2014: 197–99. Print.

Glasstone, Richard. "The Influence of Cecchetti on Ashton's Work". *Following Sir Fred's Steps: Ashton's Legacy*. Ed. Stephanie Jordan and Andrée Grau. London: Dance Books, 1996. 8–13. Print.

Kirkland, Gelsey, and Greg Lawrence. *The Shape of Love*. London: Hamish Hamilton, 1990. Print.

Lewis, Frederick. "View from the Barre". *Dancing Times* 103.1228 (2012): 35–37. Print.

McCarthy, Brendan. "Beginners Ballet for Adults". *Dancing Times* 97.1156 (2006). 25–27. Print.

Plymouth Dance Academy. "Adult Ballet". *Plymouth Dance Academy*. 2013. Web. 29 May 2014. www.plymouthdanceacademy.co.uk/#!adult-ballet/c1khi

Robinson, Dan. "Classes show ballet is 'not just for girls in pink tutus'". *Oxford Mail*. 1 Mar. 2014. Web. 29 May 2014. www.oxfordmail.co.uk/news/yourtown/oxford/11045923.print/

Royal Academy of Dance. "Dance for Lifelong Wellbeing". *Royal Academy of Dance*. 3 Apr. 2014. Web. 29 May 2014. www.rad.org.uk/dflw

Schwaiger, Elisabeth. *Prelude. Ageing, Gender, Embodiment and Dance*. Basingstoke: Palgrave, 2012. ix–xii. Print.

Sitnikova, Irina. "The Russian School". A Focus on Style: the schools that inspired de Valois. Royal Ballet School. 3 Feb. 2013. Lecture Demonstration; Masterclass.

Tulle, Emmanuelle. "The Ageing Body and the Ontology of Ageing: Athletic Competence in Later Life". *Body and Society* 14.3 (2008): 1–19. Print.

Turner, Bryan S. and Steven P. Wainwright. "Narratives of Embodiment: Body, Aging, and Career in Royal Ballet Dancers". *Cultural Bodies*. Ed. Helen Thomas and Jamilah Ahmed. Oxford: Blackwell Print, 2004. 98–120. Print.

Young, Anita. "The English School". A Focus on Style: the schools that inspired de Valois. The Royal Ballet School. 17 Mar. 2013. Lecture Demonstration; Masterclass.

ROSIE GERHARD

Before becoming a lecturer in dance studies, Rosie taught modern foreign languages in secondary schools for twelve years, running a department and organising visits and exchanges abroad. After formalising her dance training, she worked for Bird College of Performing Arts tutoring dance history and analysis modules for both diploma and undergraduate degree students, as well as supervising dissertations and delivering study skills sessions. Since joining the staff of the Faculty of Education at the RAD in 2009, Rosie has built on this experience by delivering modules that focus on history and analysis but also include philosophy and combine both practice and theory.

What do Older Learners Want?

BY DR VICTORIA WATTS

My father is in his early 70s. He is still working and still actively volunteering in his community. He and my mum enjoy a very busy social life, going to parties, having dinner with friends, visiting the theatre. I don't think of my parents as old or frail in any way. And although they might complain of the odd ache or pain, and joke about not being as young as they used to be, they do not really think of themselves as 'old' either: in all likelihood they will be furious that I am even mentioning them when writing about older learners. They enjoy using technology in order to video chat with me when I am living abroad and to share with their friends photos, videos, links to internet 'funnies', they both joined Facebook some time ago, and they play the new generation of games on their mobile devices. My dad is the person who got me hooked on Angry Birds a few years ago. My mum introduced me to Candy Crush Saga. They still provide a significant amount of practical support to their middle-aged children.

Why start with this mini family portrait? So often the headlines about demographic shift, about increasingly aged populations within the privileged economies of the world, are constructed in terms of 'burden' and 'sustainability' only thinly veiling an underlying ageism. News reports largely fail to acknowledge the contribution the over-65s make to their communities and to the economy. And they cast older people as somehow 'other', struggling with technology and other facets of the modern world, with age often connoting a necessary and inevitable diminishing of mental and physical capacity. Like many people, I can fall prey to an easy reliance on these kinds of stereotypes. They play into my own fears about ageing. However, when I look at my parents and their friends, I see how narrow the conversation about ageing can be when set against the very diverse, often very rich, experiences of older people.

My understanding of the diversity of people in the older age groups in the UK was enhanced through my work project managing the RAD's Dance for Lifelong Wellbeing initiative.[1] This became a transformative project for nearly everyone who was involved and engendered a broad set of outcomes in relation to teaching,

---

[1] A more detailed description of the project, our research method and initial analysis of date, and a host of resources for teachers can be downloaded for free: www.radeducation.org.uk/danceforlifelongwellbeing

professional development and wellbeing, many of which we are still analysing.

In the report published immediately following the conclusion of the project, the RAD team concentrated primarily on discussing findings that addressed the needs of teachers who might want to extend their practice to include working with older adults. The voices of teachers who participated in the pilot study come across very clearly, but the voices of our older learners are less apparent, even though we sought to make sure they were heard within the planning and delivery of the project itself. In this essay I am going to take the opportunity to redress that balance somewhat and give some space to our findings about what older learners want when they participate in a dance class. First though, I will give some background for this discussion by giving an overview of the Dance for Lifelong Wellbeing project and by showing how this work (the pilot project, ongoing RAD initiatives, and discussion of 'student voice' when those students are older adults) is so important given national and international contexts with respect to ageing populations.

Assumptions on ageing

It is widely predicted that by 2015 there will be more people on the planet over the age of 60 than there are children under the age of 14 (*International Facts*). It is already the case that more people in the UK are aged over 65 than under 18. In the next twenty years the number of people here over 85 is expected to double. It is a dramatic rate of increase. Yet the population in the UK is ageing more slowly at the moment than in many comparable countries. No wonder governments around the world are alarmed: they wonder whether social welfare and healthcare systems can cope with the demands that more people (whom they see as economically unproductive and physically frail) will place on them. This fear stems from a belief that an ageing population is necessarily a drain on a country's resources and that the elderly contribute nothing in return. Indeed, much of the discourse on ageing and wellbeing appears to rest on an assumption that ageing is a problem that needs to be solved.

Alex Dumas, in a sociological analysis of ageing, points out that quite pervasive anti-ageing practices connected to health, beauty and wellbeing are "strongly connected to people's accepting of the idea that to age well is not to age at all" (376).

In light of the condescending attitudes many people exhibit towards older adults, those characterised as 'third agers' or, when even older, as being in the 'fourth age', I can well understand why so many people are keen to mask all visible signs of ageing. But surely it is possible to work with older learners in ways that approach ageing positively rather than attempting to hide it or deny its inevitability? Even the literature that seeks to address wellbeing and ageing can slip into a rather patronising 'othering' of elders. In her report on exercise, ageing, and self-concept (by which she broadly means self-esteem), Sherrill Berryman-Miller concludes:

"An underlying message for the older adult is that the responsibilities of self-care are a part of retirement. A retired person who must abandon the work ethic may replace it with a conscientious concern for health and independence." (43–44)

Doubtless, it is a well-intentioned remark, but it reads as though the author thinks adults over 60 or 65 need to be tasked with taking care of themselves or else, released from the demands of the workplace, they will simply let themselves go and spend the day watching TV, eating junk, and waiting for social services to drop by and clean the house for them. I am reminded of a nugget of wisdom from my own teacher, Susan Hadley, who was preparing graduate students to teach in the Dance Department at The Ohio State University. She emphasised that although our students may well be new to dance classes they would likely have a wealth of experience in other areas. Just because they were beginning dancers they were not also beginning people. Clearly this is an important attitude to adopt when working with older adults.

Setting aside problematic stereotypes about older people, it is known that participation in physical activity diminishes as people progress through various phases of life. Only 7% of the over 75 age group reports participating

[2] The various Departments of Health across the four countries of the UK have issued a set of factsheets on the recommendations for physical activity that can be accessed for free from this website: www.gov.uk/government/publications/uk-physical-activity-guidelines.

in the minimum levels of physical activity recommended for health benefits (Later Life in the UK 5). Falls, often as a result of the loss of the kind of 'physical reserve' we all have when younger (Avers 275) can be devastating for the over 65s and represent more than half of all admissions to hospital for accidental injury (Later Life in the UK). In his report on community-based exercise programmes for older people, Dale Avers emphasises the importance of taking action before this loss of physical reserve begins to affect functional capacity (275). In other words, adults of all ages should be attempting to meet the guidelines on minimum levels of physical activity to maintain good health.[2] It has also been widely reported that participation in various forms of dance class can have a positive impact on maintenance of cognitive function. It is noteworthy that in the BUPA Report 'Keep Dancing' compiled by the Centre for Policy on Ageing, the aggregated studies on which they draw appear to show that many of the benefits appear to be correlated with amateur dance activity throughout adulthood rather than the specific uptake of dance in later life.

Dance for Lifelong Wellbeing

One of the major problems older adults in disadvantaged communities face when it comes to meeting any recommendations on physical activity is access to good quality dance or exercise programmes led by professionals who understand how to tailor their teaching practice to suit a wide range of learners. It was in order to meet this need that the

RAD's Faculty of Education initiated the Dance for Lifelong Wellbeing project. Supported by a grant from the Community Learning Innovation Fund (CLIF) and administered by the National Institute for Adult Continuing Education (NIACE), it combined a small-scale qualitative research project on the impact of dance classes on wellbeing, with community outreach across London, and a series of workshops and mentoring for dance teachers who were keen to expand their practice working with adults at the same time as developing skills as practitioner researchers. Over the course of six months, a small team in the Faculty of Education at the RAD, supported by Dr Victoria Showunmi from the Institute of Education and Clare Guss-West, devised a programme of events, classes, focus groups, and data collection to achieve our rather ambitious set of goals: six teachers working across 12 venues, reaching over 100 older learners and sharing insight on our practices across the RAD network.

A key component of our bid for the grant money was the focus on consultation with all the various stakeholders in both devising and evaluating the project. An important element of this process was the Project Evaluation Day conducted at the RAD's headquarters in Battersea at the conclusion of the community outreach phase. Representatives of our older learners from each of the community venues attended and gave us frank feedback on all elements of the programme through a series of focus groups co-ordinated by Dr Showunmi.

Five key findings emerged from our consultation in relation to what our participants wanted from a dance class and what they had valued most from taking part in the pilot study.

More of the same, please

Learners talked a lot about the ways in which initiatives of all sorts were often funded for just a very short time. The words of one participant resonate strongly on this point: "They give us something good only to take it away again."

Our pilot study offered older learners a six-week course of classes that they could attend for free. The feedback we received was resoundingly clear: that learners wanted these classes as a permanent feature of their weekly activities. The challenge for community venues and nursing homes, for teachers, and for older learners, is then how to make these classes sustainable over the long term.

We asked learners about whether or not they would be able or willing to contribute to the cost of their classes. Our learners were from relatively disadvantaged communities in South London but nevertheless most said they would be prepared to pay between £2 and £5 per class. Others suggested a sliding scale, with learners paying according to means.

Collaborating with several of the partners from the Dance for Lifelong Wellbeing project, the Faculty of Education successfully bid for grant funding to continue classes in Wandsworth for another year, ensuring that teachers could be paid for their work, that appropriate teaching spaces could be hired, and that learners could continue to attend free of charge. Across the UK there are various small pots of money available from local councils and small charities to support these kinds of community learning and wellbeing projects. It may be that teachers who have begun working in this area and discovered how rewarding it can be will want to volunteer an hour of their time for a good cause. I have been doing just this at a nursing home near my new home town of Adelaide, Australia. I give a 45 minute session to residents who are, for the most part, chair-bound, many of whom are already suffering from cognitive impairment. It is a very small part of my week but it makes a big difference to the learners and to the care staff at the nursing home.

Progression

Several participants in the focus group sessions mentioned that they enjoyed the sense of progression in their learning. Of course, it is hard to build this effectively over just six weeks, but learners noted how satisfying it was to find that from week to week they could see an improvement in their skills as they practised creative tasks, or were able to correctly perform the timing of a routine, or found they could balance more easily, turn without getting dizzy, move their fingers and wrists with greater ease. RAD teachers all learn about the importance of planning for progression. This is no less important with older adults than it is with young teenagers who might be preparing to enter an exam or take part in a big performance.

It came as something of a surprise to find that one or two of our focus group participants even requested work to take home. This could take many different forms, depending on the particular needs and abilities of the group. A teacher might ask participants to practice one particular exercise or movement for the next class. For example, seated participants with some movement in their lower bodies might be encouraged to practice toe and heel taps or extensions of the lower leg every day in order to help maintain strength. For other groups, especially those who are responding well to creative tasks, giving out a poem to read (printed in a large font for ease of reading) and tasking learners with choosing one line and creating a gesture or a motif to share with others in the next class, would be an appropriate homework task. Or, if learners are working a set routine it might be worthwhile sharing a copy of the music so they can practice at home between classes. It might also be that if the class is focused on a particular genre of dance, such as tap, learners might be eager to read, watch or hear more about the history of the dance form.

A strong sense of community cohesion

Everyone involved in the project across all our community partners commented on the sense of community built up through participation in these group dance classes. It was noted that there seemed to be better bonds between participants, especially in places where learners had been attending regularly for years but only ever sitting with the same people, talking about the same things. The social element of the dance activities had

forged new connections and given new things to talk about. It was clear to our teachers that the dance classes also seemed to shift the relationships between care workers and learners within nursing homes and day care centres. Having support staff also participate in classes provided a new point of connection and a shared experience of fun. It was our learners within the most independent classes, those who signed up to participate not necessarily knowing anyone else who would come along, who commented most strongly on the value of building community through participation.

New research suggests that good social relationships are as important for long life and general wellbeing as a healthy diet, regular exercise and abstention from smoking (Davidson, Goodwin & Rossell). It is then not merely an ancillary benefit if participation in dance class can improve social bonds for learners. Quite probably, it is as vital as any gains in balance, strength, and cognitive agility. These social bonds may happen without the teacher actively choosing to support them.

Above: A session from the RAD's older adults project. Photo credit Robert Griffin.

For example, a ballet class can offer few opportunities for social interaction between learners but adults still often make new friends through their participation.

Nonetheless, teachers can be instrumental in developing this sense of community through their choice of activities and the way they structure the entire learning experience. Our teachers often incorporated name games, ice breakers and social interaction into their warm-up activities. They made use of group learning activities and created an atmosphere in which learners felt free to chat and joke during some of the activities. In some venues, time for water or juice breaks were an opportunity for socialising and in some this went further to include time for cakes and cups of tea. In every instance, our teachers made a point of chatting with learners before or after class in order to get to know them better. This dimension of the practice was valued by learners and teachers alike.

Fun

The overriding message from participants was that the thing they valued most about the classes was the sense of playfulness, creativity and fun. Dances with sparkly hats, games with feathers, and exercises with ribbons or pom-poms seemed to give permission to learners to tap into a freer, less serious way of inhabiting their bodies. When conducting an observation of one of the sessions I was struck by a sudden impression of youthfulness among the participants as they joked and giggled and misbehaved while trying a movement

game with a balloon. There was nothing childish about this. Rather it seemed to be a manifestation of ebullience. Other studies have commented on the way in which participation in dance can seem to transcend everyday experiences of the ageing body. For example, Helen Thomas and Leslie Cooper noted this phenomenon in their study of social dancers in South East England:

> "The capability of dancers almost literally to put down their crutches and dance suggests also that the body is more than an aggregate of mechanical parts that either work or break down. It is a lived experiential body, which, for a short time at least, can be transcended so that its predominant defining characteristics, in this case disability and fatigue, are forgotten in the pleasure of the dance" (705).

This marries with Krishnavelli Kathleen Nadesen's findings during her study of older women's participation in line-dancing in South Africa. When questioned, these women attested that in dancing they forgot about their age (12). Moreover Nadesen judges from her data that the primary impetus for attending line dancing classes was "the 'enjoyment and fun aspects' and the 'perceived benefits' were the natural outflows of the various activities involved in line dancing" (13). Likewise, our learners were very clear that they come to class because they want to have fun. Other benefits accrue from this total absorption in the art of dancing, playing, and creating, but the opportunity to experience joy is essential.[3]

More men

No one involved in the project was shocked to find that roughly 90% of our older learners were female. We know women tend to live longer than men, and we know that for a very long time participation in dance classes has been regarded as a more suitable activity for girls and women. However, during the focus group sessions, both men and women who had taken classes said they would like to see more men getting involved. From the women, this assertion was often accompanied by some saucy laughter or a wink. And why not? Dance classes such as these are a good way to make new friends.

Professionalism and a brand you can trust

It did come as a surprise to the project team to hear how much it mattered to participants that these classes were being offered by the Royal Academy of Dance. Affiliation with a respected dance organisation lent credibility, in the minds of our learners, to the project. Venue partners

[3] I think there is a connection between this absorption in a pleasurable task, in learners' ability to transcend the aches, pains, and limitations of the body, and what phenomenologist Drew Leder discusses in his book *The Absent Body*. He makes the case that we are most aware of our bodies when we are in pain, trying to learn a new physical skill, or are feeling socially self-conscious. Our attention is drawn to the body itself and our feelings of discomfort at times like these. By contrast, under ordinary circumstances we are using our bodies to attend to the world, to whatever task we are absorbed in. It is no wonder that when we are caught up in the flow of a pleasurable activity, one in which we feel a joyful ease, our perception of bodily pain and limitation might lessen.

thought that the RAD 'brand' made it much easier to recruit participants than they would otherwise have expected. A corollary to the credibility given by the RAD was the professionalism of our teachers. They inspired confidence in the learners and made them feel secure. Undoubtedly, taking up a dance class (or any new activity) can be daunting no matter what age you are. Our learners said they felt as though they were in safe hands because of the professionalism of our volunteers and the affiliation to a brand they felt they could trust.

Conclusion

Our data seems to show that what older learners value in a dance class differs very little from what any adult wants in a recreational dance class. Emphases on fun, creativity, continuity and community appeared very strongly in our focus group data, in teachers' reflective journals, in lesson observations, and in video footage. Certainly, teachers working with older adults need to be aware of the range of physical and cognitive capabilities this population might bring to class. More than that, teachers need to appreciate that older learners are much like any other kind of learner and that a student-centred approach to teaching, a sense of play, and a willingness to let go of preconceived ideas about the elderly provide an excellent foundation for beginning to work in this field.

When we began the Dance for Lifelong Wellbeing project, I convinced my Mum to travel down to London to participate as a dancer in one of the initial training workshops.

Clare Guss-West wanted our project teachers to experience working with older adults before they began their community placements, so we had an afternoon of shared practice with teachers, older learners and project facilitators all following Clare's lead. Mum brought a friend with her and they both reported having a marvellous day out and really enjoying the dancing. I have heard from her several times since what a shame it is that nothing comparable is on offer where she lives. Although I'm still working hard to convince my dad that he should find the time to do a bit more exercise, I know that there are many people just like my mum who would jump at the chance to join in a fun dance class. So, if anyone in Buckinghamshire wants to set up a fun, sociable dance class for the 60+ age group, please let me know and I'll send my mum and her friends in your direction.

References

Avers, Dale. "Community-Based Exercise Programs for Older Adults". *Topics in Geriatric Rehabilitation* 26.4 (2010): 275–98. Print.

Berryman-Miller, Sherrill. "Dance/Movement: Effects on Elderly Self-Concept". *Journal of Physical Education, Recreation & Dance* 59.5 (1988): 42–46. Print.

Centre for Policy on Ageing. "Keep Dancing… The Health and Wellbeing Benefits of Dance for Older People". BUPA, 2011. 1–20. Print

Cooper, Leslie and Helen Thomas. "Growing Older Gracefully: Social Dance in the Third Age". *Ageing and Society* 22.6 (2002): 689–708. Print.

Davidson, Susan, James Goodwin and Phil Rossall, eds. *Improving Later Life. Understanding the Oldest Old.* London: Age UK, 2013. Print.

Dumas, Alex. "Rejecting the Ageing Body". *The Routledge Handbook of the* Body. Bryan S. Turner. Ed. London: Routledge, 2013. 375–388.

Factsheet 5: Physical Activity Guidelines for Older Adults (65+). UK: Department of Health, 2011. Print.

International Facts. London: Age UK, 2011. Print.

Later Life in the United Kingdom: December 2013. London: Age UK, 2013. Print.

Leder, Drew. *The Absent Body.* Chicago: The University of Chicago Press, 1990. Print.

Nadasen, Krishnavelli Kathleen. "Perceived Health Benefits of Line Dancing for Older Women" *Quality in Ageing* 8.3 (2007): 4–14. Print.

"Physical Activity Guidelines for Older Adults". British Heart Foundation National Centre. Web. 17th January 2014. www.bhfactive.org.uk/olderadultsguidelines/index.html

VICTORIA WATTS

Victoria Watts works as a Lecturer in Arts Education at the University of South Australia in Adelaide where she also serves as Secretary of Australian Fulbright Alumni Association for the state. In her former role with the Royal Academy of Dance she led the pilot programme of the Dance for Lifelong Wellbeing project and she continues to research best practice in provision of dance classes for older learners through ongoing collaborations with colleagues in London. Qualified to Advanced level in Benesh Movement Notation and Labanotation, her parallel research focus attends to the theorizing of dance notation practices and related questions of embodied knowledge. She holds an MFA in Dance (with a concentration in technology) from the Ohio State University and a PhD in Cultural Studies from George Mason University.

Free the Spirit

BY VERONICA HORWELL

It couldn't have been a bleaker afternoon out on an estate in Roehampton, London, famed for its lack of cheer. The local church hall wasn't that uplifting a venue either, although the dozen or so souls, just one of them male, who didn't put on their coats to leave after the weekly pensioners' lunch in the hall were in blithe enough spirits. The lunch had been very nice, thank you, but they had come for the dancing, a bonus session to a series of classes back in the winter. They had saved their energy all week for this, and welcomed Lynn Blackman, their teacher, like ballet-struck 'bunheads'. Let's get moving, Lynn.

Not that moving necessarily meant stepping out. Half the group, their legs or balance iffy, sat on chairs in a row, very Bob Fosse, just the arms and feet jiggling in the warm-up routine to 'We'll take Manhattan'. Lynn had been uncertain at the start of the classes what choreography her pupils might have in common, if any, but they were all of an age – well, a span of ages, 70s to 95 – to share basic showbiz as a body language, and over the weeks they had got this little chorus line routine going. 'Manhattan' segued into 'Together': for those who were on their feet, step, turn,

beat with a kick implied by its absence, circle, reverse. They put on professional show smiles – sell it, babes – halfway through the first number, but were smiling for real by the second. Dance lightens the heart even faster than the step. They were being, for the moment, who they had always been: regular dancers.

The Roehampton sessions had emerged from a popular reminiscence group, in which a great, cross-background experience of the 20th century had turned out to be 'going dancing'. The mode and venue of the experience hadn't been standardised: between them, this line-up had foxtrotted at the Hammersmith Palais de Danse in the era of Astaire and Rogers, jitterbugged with US servicemen in the Lyceum Ballroom in the West End, and jived at the Locarno, Streatham: they had practised in back courts and sculleries if there was nowhere else uncluttered, and dressed up when possible (Doris Atkins once reached a dance hall in bare feet, to save her good shoes for the main event). There had been cigarette stubs underfoot up the Palais, but chandeliers overhead – like the foyers of Odeon picture palaces, the premises of a palais were aspirational, fantasyland – and the bands played live right up to rock'n'roll. Maria Taylor took classes as a teen in Wandsworth Town Hall in the early 1930s so she could manage the tango at afternoon tea dances: the tango was the most committed of dances, only attempted by the serious. The dreariness of Phyllis Gibson's wartime factory labour was livened up by friends who returned from rare excursions up to town having learned a few new steps, and shared them with the other girls – a free luxury, a novelty that needed no rationed materials, to be tried out to *Workers' Playtime* on the radio.

Don't imagine the Roehampton dancers immobilised by nostalgia in their session. I had to grab the memories on the hop, after those on their feet had executed a stroll-by on 'Me and My Shadow'. They wanted to talk about dancing now, too, how much it meant to them. Phyllis also still did tap, and country dancing, and performed in a church hall show. Maria (well on her way to her centenary) said: "I like watching *Strictly*, but it's all too acrobatic now, it's not social anymore." After the tango became passé, her favourite Latin routine had been the rumba, and she gave a delicate little tremor of alternating shoulders to demonstrate its subtle sexiness. Pamela Emmanuel, another Hammersmith veteran (she had met her husband there), was happy to be moving at all after two heart attacks. Evelyn Pegg had had two knee replacements a few months ago, "and my chief worry was that I wouldn't be back at the dance sessions. I live for dancing." But she was not only swaying on the chair line, blissed-out, but dancing again

in her kitchen at home, "dancing in with my lunch on a tray. It's good for the soul."

That willing all-body movement, plus a restoration of sociability, in service of wellbeing had been the formal purpose of the experimental dance sessions, and satisfied Victoria Watts, who was at that time Head of Global Education Partnerships at the RAD, who was monitoring the gig. Watching the dancers, I could see other benefits not perhaps in Victoria's original mission statement. How sharp they all were, even the frailest, and unembarrassed by error: there was still time to get things right by repetition, and relaxed human contact in getting them wrong – they set each other on the correct path. Dance permits people to exist physically, gives them a reason and a way to present a self to the world. The young demand that, and will grab it if it isn't granted, but permission for a body just to be is withdrawn as we age: we are supposed to withdraw ourselves from the body into the cave of the mind.

Afterwards, Victoria and I waited for a bus out of the estate, and aboard she explained that as part of her job, she kept up to date with broad cultural trends in dance education. She had been struck by an EU information directive on demographics, which made it clear that Europe's supply of child pupils was diminishing and would dwindle further, and with it the livelihoods of present and future dance teachers, while the potential pairs of feet aged 60 and over multiplied annually. Social demographics – what differing age groups are prepared to do by habit and custom – suggested that the willingness of the young to be glum alone at the gym in search of whatever it is they're in search of (strength through boredom, probably, not a lot of joy about) wasn't shared by their elders, who are not working towards the goal of a thinner, fitter tomorrow: half an hour's good time now will do more for their wellbeing. Much discussion and several proposals later, Victoria had money through the Skills Funding Council and the Community Learning Innovation Fund for an experiment, and offered teachers for sessions in age centres, clubs like Roehampton, even care homes. It had been a risk, she said. It seemed a promising idea, but would anybody actually get up and dance?

The bus doors opened, and on jumped one of our dancers, who – while we had stood stiff as boards in the biting wind at the terminus – had walked briskly to the next bus stop but two, still bouncy on her soles. We felt feeble. Victoria was vindicated.

Next day the revived dance class at the Hestia Centre in Tooting clustered round their teacher, Helen Linkenbagh, patting and stroking her like a beloved pet. Bet she doesn't get that from her other pupils. Hestia's menfolk were booming away upstairs at the card tables, so the class was again a dozen women, once from worlds wider than South London: only Lilian Macartney cited Hammersmith Palais as the location for her youthful Terpsichore: "I jumped through the window at home one night, got up there to jive with the Americans, then got thrown out."

All the teachers in the experiment had been allowed to choose their own music and create their own programme. Helen had gone not

outwards, like Lynn – "Smile, babes, wave" – but inwards. She warmed them up by pretending to knead bread, then had them improvise to dreamy music – a return in the mind to any place where they had been happy long ago, to mime bringing back… what? A mango. A lime. A fish. A bunch of flowers out of the fields. Turtle eggs. Mabel Headley went back to the Barbados that she so missed: "Blue sky. I went straight there to the beach, bunches of coconuts." They circled and swam in warm waters and stretched arms to a sun that wasn't shining in Tooting – not dance as an entertainment but as an exploration of self.

Helen had originally worried that they might be nervous about prancing about and being grasshoppers in a wheat field, but her class wasn't inhibited ("they should grab it with open arms," said Mabel), although one or two had had to wait a lifetime for a chance to hit the floor. Glo Shiromani, who had been brought up by nannies in a remote colonial world so formal she had to be chaperoned to

Above: A session from the RAD's older adults project. Photo credit Robert Griffin.

Projects, Profiles, Perspectives

Above: A session from the RAD's older adults project. Photo credit Robert Griffin.

go to the cinema, confessed, "I never danced like this. My friend pulled me by the hair and brought me here, I thought I had two left feet. I'm catching up. I didn't know I could reach the floor with my hands flat." "You coming out, gal!" encouraged Mabel, who, bad back notwithstanding, needed no encouragement – fully signed up for tai chi, zumba, gospel singing, any movement going: "Honey, if you whistle, we dance." Rhythm and blues animated her when young and she'd done it all – ballroom, square dancing, and maypole.

Despite Helen's different approach, the same good humour broke out when the class attempted a cha-cha in formation. The shy Clarrie Chisum's hips started to swing: "It take you right back to childhood." The dancers collided and failed to meet, but that only made it more fun, like family games, hours and days of only voices and bodies to make amusement. Where the Roehampton dancers had taken their chance to be stylishly young again, remembering their personas of attraction, the Hestia gals were after the

pleasure of being actively embodied, living in the sinews, which we give up when we put away childish things.

Like children, they didn't want it to end, even though they were beginning to heat up and wilt. Helen had to go, it was a long journey home to her toddler son, but not before everyone had hugged her, and each other, and begged for more lessons: Glo didn't want to seize up, stiffen, freeze on her knees, to stop dancing as she prepared the veg in her kitchen. Helen's teachers' group had told the instructors what to aim for with their older pupils – balance, flexibility, core stability – but she was surprised at what those solid women in their 70s, even 80s, could do, although not as surprised as they were themselves. A dancer had called "free the spirit" as she moved down the floor – it's a gospel invocation to unblock resistance to a power greater, and more benign, than your conscious, controlling mind. Maybe free the body, too: same thing. "We weren't always old," said Lilian, who danced very lightly, and could keep it up. "Enjoy it now," advised Mabel. "You never know what tomorrow may bring."

This article was first published under the pen name, Vera Rule, in Dance Gazette (Issue 2; 2013), the RAD's magazine.

VERONICA HORWELL
Veronica Horwell is a journalist and essayist; she writes regularly for the Guardian, and has written for a wide range of publications from Le Monde Diplomatique through Vogue to The International Journal of Naval History. Her answer to many of life's minor woes is a quick, secret dance session to Cole Porter's Begin the Beguine.

In Conversation: Elaine Giles and Helen Linkenbagh

Helen was one of the six teachers and Elaine one of the participants in the RAD's pilot research and outreach project on dance and wellbeing for older adults.

HELEN: Elaine, how did you first discover the Dance for Lifelong Wellbeing classes?

...

ELAINE: I discovered one of those striking yellow *Dance for Lifelong Wellbeing* flyers advertising free classes for older adults. I signed up with a group of friends, all local Battersea (London) residents, who were keen to take up the opportunity to participate. I attended two 'phases' of classes, your classes at the RAD and the classes with Hannah Bailes at the Katherine Low Centre. I've continued to dance in classes for the last year.

...

HELEN: What were your first impressions of the class?

...

ELAINE: We were all given a very warm welcome; there were chairs set out and we were offered refreshments. We also felt very much as if we could do as much or as little of the class as we liked. We also appreciated that the RAD had asked about any physical limitations we might have, and had given us a health questionnaire so as to be able to accommodate each person's needs.

The session itself was immensely enjoyable and very positive. The creative task we performed (exploring the imagery from a poem) immediately tapped into positive memories of childhood; pleasurable memories such as baking bread. I was able to go to a place from my youth and was immediately blown away by the beauty. I felt I could hear birds!

Since that time I don't recall any other experience – not even reading poetry or novels – that has tapped into those memories in quite the same way. It was through allowing time and space, and the suggestion of moving through that place and trying to access the sensations that one had at that time – and then to interpret and express them in that way. It was a very powerful and eye-opening experience.

...

HELEN: What did you think of the teaching style of the class?

...

ELAINE: I love to see the teachers move as we work in class, the way they move the body right to the tips of the fingers and toes. It is wonderful and educational to see that and to dance with them.

Above: A session from the RAD's older adults project. Photo credit Robert Griffin.

...

HELEN: As the teacher in this instance, I can say that in ensuring that I'm dancing with a broad and open sense of embodied energy, I know that I can encourage greater energy and facilitate a greater range of movement in my students. The use of the eyes and upper body is essential in connecting with participants and communicating movement ideas and feelings, so I understand when you say this as an important aspect of the impact of the classes.

Do you feel that participating in the Dance for Lifelong Wellbeing classes has had an impact on your general state of health and mobility?

...

ELAINE: I have experienced an increase in the flexibility of my feet, toes and knees. I think that this is due to the level of detail in our warm-up where we focus on the articulation of the feet and alignment and stability through the lower legs in *plié*. This part of the class has

even contributed positively to the dreary task of waiting for the bus: I now do it all at bus stops whilst waiting – kneading bread dough with my toes!

...

HELEN: Which aspects of the class have had an effect that extends beyond the dance studio?

...

ELAINE: I love the music that we use in the classes and now look for opportunities to listen to and engage with music at home and elsewhere. All my adult life I thought I needed to learn, so I have had BBC Radio 4 on from the time I wake to the time I go to bed. I have learned a lot, but maybe it has been tiring or even over-stimulating? Being reminded how wonderful some pieces of music are and how they can change how you feel, sending you spiraling around the room and giving you tremendous energy. I thought, 'now, I have to start doing things that give me more energy and joy in my daily life'. So instead of watching TV and giving up control to what comes on, I now choose to put music on in the house.

...

HELEN: Have you noticed any other benefits from the classes?

...

ELAINE: I have had problems with my spine in the past, but feel that due to a combination of finding effective treatment and a consequent increase in confidence, I can now participate in Pilates classes and other activities, including the Dance for Lifelong Wellbeing classes. My posture and mobility has greatly increased thanks to the movements we perform in class:

gently opening and closing and spiraling the arms and upper body, with coordination of breath, opening and chest and shoulders. Along with little reminders – like when the teacher tells us that our heads are like balloons floating upwards – are really useful. This imagery is a subtle way of balancing and realigning the spine that has contributed to my regained back strength.

The tasks where we dance with feathers were a real revelation as well in terms of being reintroduced to a sense of wonder and childhood, of joyous play. The extended dance sequences that we perform at the end of each lesson help memory, confidence and security when stepping (going right, left, changing weight rapidly). The increased ability for reaction in the body and the ease of control that we gain as we work means that it never feels like a stressful situation anymore.

…

HELEN: You've now started attending a Latin/Tango class. How is that going?

…

ELAINE: Having the confidence gained from the Dance for Lifelong Wellbeing classes has made me want to do this. I have become healthier because of the treatment, and the improvement in health has been enhanced by the classes. They both came along at just the right time.

HELEN LINKENBAGH
Helen is a qualified and registered RAD teacher and was Director of her own school in New South Wales, Australia, from 1994 to 2006. A graduate of the RAD's BA in Dance Education programme, she completed a Graduate Diploma in Choreography in 2008 at the Victorian College of the Arts, Melbourne. She worked as a sessional tutor and lecturer for the Faculty of Education since 2007, and became a Lecturer in Dance Studies in September 2013. Helen teachers classical ballet, Graded and Vocational level RAD exam work and contemporary dance in London and Kent, and works as a cover teacher for the Associate Programmes at the Royal Ballet School. Helen continues to work with groups of older dance students as a part of the RAD's 'Dance for Lifelong Wellbeing' initiative.

ELAINE GILES
Elaine worked as a clinical and research Speech and Language Therapist, and manager for 30 years until Chronic Fatigue /Immune deficiency prevented it. She now balances work as a mediator for KIDS, with volunteering for the Art and Spirituality Network, and the Victoria and Albert Museum with painting, and making things. She firmly believes in the lifelong importance of communication and creativity for mental and physical wellbeing.

Growing Older – (Dis)gracefully Dance

BY JUDY SMITH

Our cheeky name affirms a playfully subversive approach to both dance and to ageing. Growing Older (Dis)gracefully, an amateur dance group of about 25 women, half of whom are over 60 (and some over 80!), exemplifies the premise that everyone can and should dance.

Some of our members had no dance experience before joining the group, others had not danced since their childhood, and a few had enjoyed long careers as dance teachers. The mix has proved magical, as the greater experience of some has inspired the others to perform with greater confidence.

Growing Older (Dis)gracefully evolved out of a 1997 initiative in Liverpool to promote active lifestyles for the over-50s. At that time, a group of dance teachers who led regular classes throughout the summer decided it would be a good idea to inspire a few volunteers to work towards a performance. *Where Past and Future are Gathered*, which has since become the company's signature work, was commissioned from a local community dance teacher, Liz Bruen, and had its first performance in December 1998.

In its early days, the dancers met whenever a performance opportunity arose. As the group's reputation grew, requests for performances became so frequent that regular rehearsal sessions were established. For the past twelve years, the company has rehearsed weekly under the auspices of the Dance Faculty of Liverpool John Moores University, who have generously supplied us with free studio space. Other than this, the company has never had any other regular funding. Occasionally, there are small contributions towards costume and travel expenses, but in the main, group members financially support their own work.

Over the past ten years, however, the company has been fortunate to secure funding from Arts4All, Arts Council North West, The Culture Company, and Liverpool City Council with the Primary Care Trust. These have enabled us to produce dance films, which have been shown at conferences nationwide, and to pay choreographers a near realistic amount for their time. Working with professional artists significantly raises the expectations of members and serves to advocate for the credibility of older person's dance.

We perform in a variety of environments locally and nationally – on local streets as well

as in more traditional theatres. Highlights of the recent past include being invited to participate in the re-opening of the Royal Festival Hall, and at national conferences in Birmingham, Gloucester and London. We were thrilled to be part the Olympic Torch celebrations and the Big Dance festivities, which culminated the Cultural Olympiad. Joining with two thousand others on the steps of Liverpool One was unbelievably inspiring.

Perhaps one of our most moving events was in spring 2012, when we danced with the Welsh Choral Society as part of a Titanic concert at Liverpool Cathedral. No-one will ever forget the emotional feeling we had as we moved down the aisle in semi-darkness to begin our *Journey*, as the piece was called, to the music of Corelli's *Christmas Concerto*.

Other venues have been of the less conventional variety. We were there in the Liverpool City Centre for the International Day of Dance, outside a pub in the Old Swan neighbourhood, to promote a healthy lifestyle campaign. We have also performed in a shop

Above: Growing Older (Dis)gracefully Dance performance.

window of a recycling shop and in local parks to help raise money for Age Concern and the local community. Every experience has proved rewarding.

The company's stability has underpinned its success. For the past eight years it has not been possible to take any new members – twenty-five is the maximum that can be accommodated in any dance space. Over time, the 'age' factor has become less significant, despite the fact that we are now all ten years older than when we started! The creative vision of the artists who work with us takes priority, and it's only after several rehearsals, if the dancers still cannot manage what is being asked of them, that alternations are made. One filmmaker asked us, "Do you leave age outside the studio door?" The answer was an emphatic, "Yes we do!"

We make sure that that everyone has a part to play despite previous experience. It is our firm belief that the group, together with the choreographer, must structure work so that everyone can be involved, feel confident, and look good in what they are asked to do. As one member asked after only four weeks, "Can I have a walk-on part?" And of course they did!

We meet weekly, with additional rehearsals before some performances. Sometimes meetings will be workshop-based, allowing us to enjoy a range of dance styles, others will be devoted to revising previously learned works – including provision for those who were not there the first time – and yet others will be used for creating new works.

One of the hallmarks of the company repertoire is the range of dance styles it contains. We have pieces in modern contemporary style, Asian fusion, tap, gospel and period (Tudor and 1940s), enabling us to tailor performances to particular audiences. Our commitment to using professional choreographers (preferably from the local area) has prodded the group to rise to new levels of skill and performance quality.

The fact that we are all women influences the subject matter of our repertoire. At the RAD conference on Dance for Lifelong Wellbeing, for instance, we performed *March of the Women*, based on the suffragette movement. We appreciate dancing within a female community, although there was no conscious decision to limit the group to women when it began. It just evolved that way, and we have not actively sought out men, as we feel it would change the nature of the group.

Like all dance companies, one of the biggest challenges we face is how to maintain its repertoire (in our case, very good for memory

Above: Growing Older (Dis)gracefully Dance performance.

training!). Currently we have about ten works we can bring to performance fairly rapidly, but each venue, and the availability of members, is different and requires changes to be made. The members respond remarkably well to the particular demands of each situation.

Whilst the purpose of our meetings is to create dance, the fact that we have lots of fun and laughter, enjoy camaraderie and generally feel refreshed (however physically demanding the session), cannot be underestimated. Everyday worries are replaced by concerns about which foot goes where, thus allowing the brain to forget, for a few hours, the pressures of everyday life. Our dancing inspires a feeling of community and togetherness which is reflected in our almost total commitment to rehearsals. We get some vigorous exercise, engage in rhythmic movement and are very social.

A passion for dance, remarkable physical achievement, self-esteem and pride in what we accomplish is visible to all who see us perform. Many members speak of the way in which being part of the company has helped them through stressful times, "You enter the studio door and you leave the world, your problems and your age on the other side." In our performances we hope to capture this wonderful sense of joy we have of dancing together, and spread the word that everyone should have the opportunity to dance regardless of age: age is no barrier or excuse not to dance.

Whilst it was dancing that brought us together, it is the growing friendships that keep us together. The motivation and support that the group provides has been therapeutic

for us all at one time or another. Being part of Growing Older (Dis)gracefully gives us all a great sense of wellbeing and achievement – that is why we are still going strong after 16 years!

JUDY SMITH

Judy has been involved in dance education all of her working life, firstly as a teacher in school and then as a lecturer (at I.M.Marsh Campus of Liverpool John Moores University), involved with training students for teaching dance both in school and in wider community contexts. During this time she was also greatly involved with the design, implementation and monitoring of GCSE dance, enabling her to share her passion for engaging everyone in some kind of dance beyond the confines of one institution.

On retirement, working with Growing Older (Dis)gracefully Dance was a natural progression. Judy feels very privileged to be able to play her part in enabling them to realise some of their dreams.

Dancing to Keep the Mind Fresh

MIRA KAUSHIK OBE

From its early days as a provider of evening classes to its transformation into a touring company in the mid to late 1980s, Akademi has cultivated enthusiasm for Indian dance. It was founded in 1979 by the eminent Indian dancer, Tara Rajkumar, who aspired to take classical Indian dance into the UK mainstream. She managed to inspire the late Robin Howard (founder of the Contemporary Dance Trust) and Naseem Khan (founder of Minority Arts Advisory Service and writer of *The Arts Britain Ignores*) to join her in setting up the Academy of Indian Dance. Its mission was to promote the development, appreciation and understanding of classical Indian dance in the social, educational and artistic context of the UK.

The Academy was the first organisation set up to deal solely with Indian dance in London. In the 1990s, we changed our name to Akademi and have since blossomed into a fully-fledged arts development organisation. This is reflected in the creation of the separate and complementary departments of education, community, dance training and dance development. The breadth of our engagement has enabled the South Asian dance aesthetic to become part of the British artistic DNA, culture and creative economy.

Arriving from the world of cinema, theatre, media and community art, I joined Akademi in the late 80s as its director. Until then, it was predominately a classical dance organisation that produced shows and ran an evening dance school. I sensed that Akademi could broaden its horizons and attract a wider audience by also engaging in South Asian dance, and so I steered the organisation into new directions by streamlining its departments in support of large scale, site-specific, professional productions and setting up the faculty of South Asian dance at the Imperial Society of Teaching of Dance (ISTD). The Education department was designed to bring South Asian dance into schools around the UK, with a long term goal of incorporating it into the mainstream curriculum, while the Community department focused on bringing South Asian dance to the local community. The two merged in 2001 to form the Education and Community department, which we have today. Our twin-track approach enables the Education and Community division to work symbiotically with our Production, Training and Professional Development unit.

Opposite: Photo credit Peter Schiazza.

Akademi maintains a heavy focus on providing South Asian dance artists in the UK with the tools and knowledge needed to forge a career through their work. Currently, through open auditions, we select talented artists to enter our Arts Development Programmes, Daredevas and Navodit for example. These offer mentoring, workshops and guidance, culminating in performances at some of London's most popular venues, such as the Southbank Centre and Rich Mix.

Mentoring is not only provided on the dance front, but also in developing business acumen in areas such as marketing and stagecraft. The artists are from a classical background but they work within the landscape of contemporary arts in Britain, and they are all kept on the Akademi radar. As a production company, we are often commissioned to produce dance pieces for events both social and corporate. We offer these to the artists we know would fit the bill, giving them a chance to showcase their work and gain wider exposure.

The Education and Community department continues to work within schools and the local community, not only to continue the stewardship ethos of Akademi, but also to raise the profile of an often unknown branch of dance.

Initiatives for Older Adults

The development of programmes specifically for older adults has become a key aspect of Akademi's outreach initiatives. My interest in this area of work stemmed from my farewell party at the Greenwich Asian Women's Arts Group, where I was asked by a care home worker if I was ever going to return to work with them. In my enthusiasm, I agreed to look into this and realised that there was no scope for this sort of provision at Akademi. So I began a process of re-invention within the organisation to find aspects of Indian dance which could be relevant to an aging population.

I worked with Pushkala Gopal, who helped us to bring yoga, breathing exercises and softer dance movements to this demographic. This experience led us to work, over the last 20 years, in a variety of environments where Indian dance, Tai Chi, Yoga, martial arts, music, literature, theatre, folk dance and Bollywood has been used in our work with many community groups.

All our work is bespoke, created to coincide with the social, cultural, physical, spiritual and mental needs of the groups we are working with. Currently we are working on the issue of Moner Khushi, meaning 'My Desire', which deals with choices and happiness during the later years of life. We also have the Bollywalk project, which encourages health and fitness in older adults through walking with Bollywood music and movement accompaniment. Our Ageing Artfully project further promotes both healthy eating and dance. This stemmed from a series of community workshops and activities for older adults in Camden, London. Working in partnership with the Surma Centre in West Euston and Camden's Active Health team, we ran innovative learning days. These encouraged and developed learning in adults, offering

inclusive opportunities to support wellbeing and included cooking for health, health walks and dance and movement workshops.

Akademi has sought to explore how and why South Asian dance can be particularly appropriate for and appealing to older adults. We collaborated, for instance, with The Bengali Worker's Association (BWA), Nexos Latinoamericanos and University Campus Suffolk (UCS) to conduct research into the effects of South Asian dance on older adults.[1] The findings suggested that South Asian dance can have a significant, positive

impact on this sector of the population. The participants in the research engaged in both movement and language-based activities, integrating dance, vivid storytelling, reminiscence work and theatre play. Realising the potential of South Asian dance and its ability to joyfully stimulate the body and mind, they reported that they felt dance "kept [the] mind fresh" and brought "happiness

[1] Akademi Inter Action Report www.akademi.co.uk/ what-we-do/resources/education-and-community-resources/tools

Above: Bisakha Sarkar performing at the RAD conference 2013.

of … mind." Clearly such a stimulating and creative dance form has many physical and mental benefits to older adults.

This is not to suggest that older adults should dance in isolation from younger generations. Akademi offers many dance/literature/music-related workshops which bring together dancers of all ages, and we have found that such inclusive, intergenerational opportunities trigger memories and a positive sense of nostalgia for the older population:

> "For we senior members it was a great privilege to take part and enjoy this late flowering in our 'careers', meeting a new dance style, and more importantly meeting these lively, lovely young dancers, creating a mixing of nations, creeds and cultures for better integration and understanding, one of your great aims in community work was well realised."
> – Elsie and Geoff McGarry (Lilian Baylis Over-60s group members)

In contrast to dance genres which tend to retire dancers at a relatively young age, South Asian dance embraces the ageing process. In South Asian culture, an artist is like a bottle of wine or a sack of rice: the more mature the better! By the time artists are noticed, they are already 40 years old, so they spend the rest of their lives working to establish themselves.

Aging is an inescapable reality. In many cultures, however, you are expected to behave yourself and be less frivolous as you age. The expression of dance is consequently one of the last forms of activity older people take on.

Yet, in the cultures with established norms of social dancing, there is more scope for dancing at an older age without any embarrassment or judgement. I feel very positive about all the ground-breaking work of Akademi. We have made great strides to challenge the negative cultural associations with aging and to break down social barriers. I am also proud to celebrate the work of our key senior artist, Bisakha Sarkar, who was awarded an MBE this year for her work with the community.

I believe dance and movement is intrinsic to our lives. Like oxygen, it allows the mind, body and spirit to breathe and flourish. My vision for Akademi is to continue to breathe life into the aging population which is ever-growing, and work to keep them connected to the world they have made for the future generations.

MIRA KAUSHIK OBE
Mira Kaushik OBE has been the Director of Akademi since 1997. Born in Belgrade (former Yugoslavia), Mira was educated at the University of Delhi, India and moved to London in 1982. With a background in literature, film, theatre and television, her professional experience includes TV and audience research for the BBC, translation, broadcasting, working with the Asian Women's Voluntary Organisation and coordinating the Festival of India at the Commonwealth Institute. Mira has overseen the production of site specific shows, including Coming of Age and Escapade at the South Bank Centre, Waterscapes at Somerset House, Sapnay, Awaz/Voice, Dreaming Now and Bells at Trafalgar Square and more recently Sufi:Zen, which toured the United Kingdom in 2010. In 2007 she was awarded an Honorary Order of the British Empire for services to dance.

Trying it for themselves: Company of Elders

BY SHEILA DICKIE

In 1989, Sadler's Wells Theatre opened its new studio performance space, the L B Theatre (now known as the Lilian Baylis Studio). To encourage local residents who were not regular theatregoers, the Community and Education department (now the Creative Learning department) had contacted retired people who lived in the vicinity and invited them to come and enjoy a cup of tea and meet some of the people who worked at the theatre. At that time, Sadler's Wells Royal Ballet were in residence and various company members offered to talk to the retirees about their work as performers. After watching a ballet class one day, the group asked if they could try it for themselves and this evolved into a regular Friday morning dance session.

Small beginnings

In 1991, when the Queen came to visit the theatre, Nadia Stern suggested that the older dancers perform for her. Choreographer Royston Maldoom was asked to devise a piece for the group, and this was so successful that it was performed again in Edinburgh and Wales.

The classes became a regular event and in due course a company was formed, initially called the 'Lilian Baylis Over 60s Performance Group'. In 1995 I became the Education Officer at Sadlers, and my role included looking after the group. As it became increasingly better known, it was invited to take part in regular dance festivals around London, arranged around its spring performance at Sadler's Wells. A pattern of producing a piece each term developed so that the work remained fresh and different. Among the early choreographers were Fergus Early, Rosemary Lee, Jamie Watton, Suz Broughton and Cheryl McChesney. Eventually it was decided to give the dancers an insight into the choreographic process and Athena Valhi came in to give them a chance to produce their own work. This process revealed some surprising hidden talent.

The company was featured in several television documentaries, including *Metroland* (1995). Years later, Alan Yentob filmed the company rehearsing for a whole term in preparation for an episode on his BBC 1 show 'Imagine' (broadcast 2009; rebroadcast in 2011 for BBC 4). Such publicity saw a deluge of interest from older people wanting to dance. It was impossible for us to satisfy the demand

and so we decided to provide outreach classes in Islington. These are still running.

During the rebuilding of Sadler's Wells, we were without our own performance space, though this provided the opportunity to move around the borough and meet other groups. Suz Broughton became the rehearsal director for those three years, giving the Company a feeling of continuity and stability.

It was during this time that Jamie Watton produced a new work for nine members of the company. Out of the 24 dancers, only eight were able to take part as they were working over four consecutive days rather than in weekly sessions. What struck me immediately was that more was achieved working in a daily intensive burst than when we had a week in between sessions. Almost an hour of each week's rehearsal was spent recapping what was learned the previous week. This lack of retention was often frustrating for choreographers who had not worked with amateur older dancers – as indeed very few had at this time.

Dance in the community

When we returned to the new Sadler's Wells in 1998, as part of the Older People's Festival, we hosted a celebration of older dancers in the borough along with Age UK Islington. We invited local groups to perform their own traditional dances from South America, India, China, Turkey and Africa, and these days of sharing cultures and dances continued for several years. Eventually we were invited, through the Gulbenkian Foundation, to

work with Clara Andermatt, a Portuguese choreographer. This became a turning point in the development of the company. Clara worked with 24 members of the group, and by this time I had managed to persuade eight men to join the company as well.

Over two weeks of intensive rehearsal, Clara encouraged the dancers to reveal their personalities and their individual histories, but at the end of the first week they were telling me that they had not yet learned any steps. I told them that Clara was very experienced and that all would be finished in time. And sure enough, by the end of the rehearsal period, a 45-minute piece had been produced. It was also the strongest work they had ever done and resulted in invitations to perform in Lagos in Portugal and, later, at the Venice Dance Biennale.

While most of the company (including me) were in Venice, the remainder were working with Luca Silvestrini, presenting a very funny piece at Ducky, a gay bar in Vauxhall, London. The piece was set in a steam room on a health farm and the dancers wore towelling gowns. The set comprised of some borrowed benches from the Rambert Dance Company – I recall making several calls from Venice to make sure they had arrived! By all accounts, the piece was very funny and the audience loved it. The company members enjoyed performing in a gay venue – we are all old men and women of the 60s. The only problem was the tiny stage, which was several feet off the ground, but thankfully no one fell off.

Opposite: Photo credit Tony Nandi.

Above: Company of Elders performing at the RAD conference 2013.

Shortly after the Ducky performance, eight dancers were invited to perform with Barbara Kane, the Isadora Duncan specialist, in Moscow. This was definitely the most trying tour to organise, but the dancers performed in some spectacular venues to a very warm reception.

The Company has been supported by successive chief executives: firstly by Ian Albery and now by Alistair Spalding, who refers to them as 'the jewel in the crown' of Sadler's Wells. Without their generous support, the Company would not be able to exist; the cost of studio hire, choreographers' fees, rehearsal director's fees and administrative costs would be far too prohibitive. The theatre raises funds for grants and the only expense to the dancers is their annual £15 membership with the Arts Club. This is open to anyone aged over 55 and the programme is usually linked to the main house performances.

A unique company

The Company of Elders is unique in that it is based in the nation's leading dance house. Dancers often work with the Associate Artists such as Hofesh Schechter, Jonzi D, Wayne McGregor and Jasmine Vardiman. In return the dancers all have to be committed to the

Company and to attend classes and rehearsals. Working with so many different choreographers has given the dancers quite a broad knowledge of contemporary dance and many of them loyally follow their favourites.

In recent years, Alistair Spalding has encouraged full-scale community performances on the main stage, and the Company of Elders has enjoyed working with a wide range of ages in these big productions.

Long-term commitment

The Company is currently formed of people aged 63-89. One member has been in the company since it began and two others have been members for over 20 years. When I ask them about what the Company means to them, their replies are extremely enthusiastic. For many it is fulfilling a lifelong ambition to dance which was denied them in their youth. Some are very nervous about performing; I recall one novice member, about to go on stage for her first performance, feeling very touched that a more experienced dancer took her hand and led her on. She retains this act of kindness, which she sees as embodying the spirit of the company.

A healthy mind in a healthy body

As far as health and wellbeing are concerned, most people are reasonably fit and some are even super-fit! What most people want is to stay as they are – we all dread the physical deterioration that inevitably happens to us as we age. From research done both here and in the USA, however, we know that the constant physical and mental stimulation involved in learning and rehearsing dance works is one of the best activities to help stave off problems affecting memory.

Of course, the other big advantage to belonging to a group or company is the companionship and friendships which develop. Loneliness is a serious problem for many older people.

Growing success

The Company of Elders continues to go from strength to strength. Such is our success that some members are even offered work with other companies: Betsy Field has danced with several other groups and Chris Dunham was offered a professional contract with Rui Horta, performing in Portugal and Brazil. Several people have also taken part in films and unusual site-specific works. It is their open-mindedness and sense of adventure keeps them trying new and exciting opportunities.

SHEILA DICKIE
Sheila trained with Nesta Bellis and Shelagh Elliott-Clarke in Liverpool and at the Royal Ballet Upper School. After several years of theatre work she ran her own school for fifteen years in north London. As a mature student she gained a BA in Dance and Education at Middlesex University and followed her interest in dance history taking an MA at the University of Surrey.

Teaching Dance History at Birkbeck, Middlesex, the Royal Academy of Dance and Hackney Community College (where she became Head of Dance), she continued her interest in the subject by joining the European Association of Dance Historians, of which she is secretary. She was Education Officer at Sadler's Wells Theatre for twelve years. She has served on various boards including the Dance Teachers' Benevolent Fund, the British Ballet Organization, Community Focus and the artsdepot. She now teaches dance and exercise to older people and dances with the Company of Elders.

Dancing the Invisible: Women Researching Ballet and Ageing Through Performance

BY JENNIFER JACKSON

This paper is a personal reflection on choreographic research into dance and ageing. The performative text and my pursuit of further research were provoked by my participation in a set of explorations at the Southbank Centre, London, initiated in 2010 by Ann Dickie, Artistic Director of the *From Here To Maturity Dance Company* (FHTM). I subsequently led in the creation of two new works, *Dancing the Invisible* and *Late Work*, both of which were developed in a highly collaborative process in 2012 at the University of Surrey by musicians and older dancers.[1]

Mapping the Terrain

Distinguished dance elders Jacky Lansley and Fergus Early[2] raise questions about perceptions of ageing and dance in their excellent collection of interviews with international artists, titled *The Wise Body*, who have maintained their dance practice

over time. In the introduction, they posit that "of all the oppressions, the one that hits dance hardest is ageism and it is the last to be explicitly addressed" (8).

Looking beyond dance, gerontologist Molly Andrews worries that, in the West, the youth and anti-ageing agenda constructs powerful models that deny society the benefits associated with ageing and maturing. In tandem these statements draw attention to the problems of dance performance focused on youth and athleticism within a culture that strives to mask the signs of ageing. If 'success' in dance is framed in terms of purely athletic spectacle, are older people excluded from participation?

In Britain, however, despite an emphasis on youth, performance by older dancers has grown substantively in the context of community dance. Arguably, audiences respond to older performers' more vulnerable physicality that reveals dimensions of human experience a highly trained body might hide.

Sadlers Wells, widely regarded as the 'National Dance House' in England, hosts the high profile *Company of Elders*. This group is something of a flagship for the numerous

---

[1] For further details of the 2012 project and performance extracts visit: http://www.surrey.ac.uk/schoolofarts/research/dance/dancingtheinvisible/index.htm

[2] Fergus Early's company Green Candle based in Bethnal Green offers regular classes and performance opportunities for older people.

Opposite: Jennifer Jackson in 'Late Work' from Dancing the Invisible production 2012. Photo credit Paul Stead.

groups operating out of dance centres and company outreach programmes whose work follows a similar model. Facilitated by professional dance practitioners, these groups give opportunities for older amateurs to explore contemporary techniques and to perform. By contrast, opportunities for older professional artists to create and develop a 'mature' dance repertoire are rare.

From Here To Maturity is then quite unique in its dedication to commissioning and programming the work of older professional dancers, who are almost invisible on the dance stage. Its 2010 research and development project brought together artists (aged 47–64) with rich experience of teaching, directing and choreographing alongside their dancing careers as independent artists and with prestigious companies such as Royal Ballet, Ballet Rambert and London Contemporary Dance Company. I was one of three women (with Lea Anderson and Ann Dickie) commissioned to lead the choreographic research.

In her choice of company name, Dickie constructs a positive view of ageing as 'maturing' and frames dancing in the process of going from here to maturity. She says that ageing:

"…is a natural process of life that everyone is involved with. And the focus is more on the physical. It has a negative flavour in our society, associated with disintegration – loss of beauty, youth and power. Mainly on loss in ours, but not in others where it is more revered. Maturing is the opposite. It

suggests fulfilment, ripening… As a process the focus in maturing is more internal and to do with the person. I guess you could say the journey of the soul. It's not to do with age." (2010 interview)

Participants in the project identified many factors that play into a dance artist's gradual self-perception of performing as a 'mature' older person and their reflections fed into the next phase of the research which took our dance to the public and on stage. Dickie points to the limited time left to the person that provokes "the urgency to speak to the essence of an idea and of saying it now" (2010). Lucy Bethune, Dickie's colleague for many years in Rambert Dance Company, suggests that an "absence of competition" generates an appreciation of what is achievable rather than pressure about what is not achievable.

Simon Rice, a virtuoso, danced principal roles with the Royal Ballet before working independently in physical theatre and education. He sees in maturing a "greater experience and awareness of yourself and others around you – and an acceptance of the 'self'" (2011 interview). Talking about her practice now, the esteemed contemporary dancer Lauren Potter remarked:

"I enjoy far more the idea of 'the moment' and less about 'choreography'. I enjoy seeing 'the human' and less 'the dancer'. I'm energised by improvisation and less by inventing 'steps and phrases of material'. Maybe this is how I visualise my 'maturing' as a performer."(Potter 2011)

After the research I reflected on the shifts over time in dancers' identities. The following themes emerged and lent focus both to a series of interviews with the participants and the creation of work in 2012: the dialectic between ageing and maturing (especially in relation to the experience of the body), virtuosity in improvisation, and diversity and collaboration.

As an older practitioner myself, I observe profound shifts in the balance between the athletic and artistic dimensions of my practice, as well as in the relationship between body and self.[3] I am interested in how this plays out in choreography and thus how mature or older dance challenges established dance performance practice, especially in ballet which is so closely associated with youthful beauty and physical virtuosity. "Where are the King Lears of dance?" asked Lea Anderson, and the roles that would enable today's audiences to reap the "reward of their [dancers'] longevity and knowledge… Dancers aren't allowed to have this experience – and it's our loss" (2011 interview).

In his book *Group Genius*, Keith Sawyer claims that it takes "a minimum of twelve years of hard work and practice before attaining a high level of performance that results in great creativity" (124). Choreography is integral to the life of ballet as a performing art: but focus on strong technique can overshadow

exploration of the more delicate expressive underpinnings of the dance. My workshops focused on these illusive parts of ballet and conceptual understanding as means of opening up formal and performative dimensions of practice in a fresh way. Using choreographic practices we explored the dancer's somatic understanding of ballet principles – the dynamic relationship of the individual's 'inner dance' with shared knowledge of 'outer' forms and practices. I found that balletic concepts provided productive frameworks for generating improvisation structures and choreographic tasks that integrate personal and disciplinary knowledge. The limitations of the ageing body operate as a creative provocation for mature professional artists. They are challenged to refine their dance 'virtuosity' through imaginative and increasingly focused practice, combining distinctiveness with collaborative skill, drawing on sensory memory and heightened awareness developed over time. Their feel for spontaneity and improvisation is grounded in the "hard work, collaboration and deep familiarity with an area" that Sawyer claims "make you more creative" (124).

My research highlighted, in particular, this capacity for collaboration – a particular acceptance of the 'self' and each other – as factors that appeared to characterise our practice as older dancers. Vera John-Steiner, writing on creative collaboration, considers the "shift in emphasis from separation to relationship" to be "the basis of self-experience and development" (105). A collective spirit or *communitas* was evoked in our processes akin

187

---

[3] For further discussion of Roger Tully's concept of the person's 'own dance' see Jackson, Jennifer. "My dance and my ideal body." *Research in Dance Education 6*, Issue 1.2 April/December (2005): 25–40

to that which Barbara Ehrenreich describes as "spontaneous love and solidarity that can arise within a community of equals" (10) reminiscent of 1960s 'happenings'. Drawing on the thoughts of my fellow researchers as well as observations of their dance practice, I wrote the following text in response to the research experience and to capture and braid the mature dance voices.

A performative text: what the older dancer knows

The older dancer brings to the creative process an embodied dialectic between her personal body of knowledge and shared bodies of knowledge. Over time she has touched upon or deeply investigated a range of ideas; some of which are embedded as muscle memory, others as fleeting emotion, affects upon her psyche. She has learnt that in the play between reflection and action in her dance, thought becomes increasingly important as her body becomes limited in its capacity to jump, turn, fly, wriggle, stretch and bend. As the movement of her limbs lessens, so the movement of thought expands. The capacities and energies of the body are known more intimately and explored with greater precision and clarity of purpose. The frameworks for understanding the discipline, its principles and practices have become increasingly clear and multi-faceted.

The dancer has explored her dance from many perspectives, each of which shines a different light on the subject and her experience. She is increasingly able to move fluidly between these perspectives and to relate the knowledge garnered in one role to explore another. She can see her dancerly knowledge in the light of her choreographic knowledge; her pedagogic in the light of her dancerly knowledge, her pedagogy in a choreographic light, and so on. She moves between experiential, practical, presentational, propositional knowing. She holds them all in her dance. She can see the place of her professional expertise threaded through the canvas of her life, recognise shifts and pivotal moments, lessons learnt. She can integrate these forms of knowledge in her artistic practice to communicate, to make work.

She is impelled by curiosity, gifts or capacities for performance and her desires. She also dances to practice wisdom, to know herself and the world. Her choices are those of the tortoise mind (Claxton) – slow, wrought over time. She knows the vulnerabilities of the body. She knows through experience of injury, she knows how to keep moving and that the body recovers but is marked. She knows the on/off of serious injury, she knows loss, she knows the gift of each moment, the present of pasts and futures embodied. She knows that when she enters a studio with 'others' with the right balance of giving and receiving, listening and speaking, something will 'happen'. She has enough under her belt to work her dance 'prose' through her intellect, or her physicality, or her emotion, or by waiting to discover which way to turn. She knows that, unlike prose, poetry is not biddable. (Kay)

She sees that with her physical body she must measure time and space more and more

precisely as she ages for her dance to be legible. She connects with the microscopic and the cosmic in her imaginative reach, evoking the vibration of the trillion cells in her body (Hay) and alignment through the force of gravity with the furthest star (Bohm). She leaps between these places invisibly in a synaptic fizz of psychic energy. Time. She sees how its patterns over her life span help her to know the ebb and flow, rise and fall, of fortune, opportunity, energy, intensity. That things pass, depart and return. She is a scientist; anxious to observe and capture the patterns, to measure and shape them in a

mirror of what she feels and experiences on multiple levels. Dancing is a way of her doing this – of reaching towards an integration of her selves and sharing her being human. She sees histories and history (Forsythe).

She sees movement in stillness and stillness in movement. She knows of the joy of dancing, the feeling of release, the merging of self into action, of being in the flow (Csikszentmihalyi). She is haunted by the memory of that extra-ordinariness and she dances to enter into that space. She recognises its provenance in a complex interrelation of personal and shared

Above: 2012 cast for Dancing the Invisible. Photo credit Paul Stead.

histories and geographies and sees how dance heightens the ephemerality and vulnerability of life itself. It drives her. She loves the way dancing connects her with others in the present, and with others in the past who have embodied the same moves that she embodies. She delights in this time travel.

She is a part of a company, an ensemble. She understands relations between the individual and the whole. She values harmony and discord. She knows isolation and conviviality in the crowd and in her own company. She knows that with a shared intention everyone can move together without a visual or audible cue – and it delights and intrigues her. She considers it as important to join with others and make dances, as it is to theorise how it happens. Each has its place. She values the contribution of each part to the whole of experience. She enjoys the freedom of moving between and settling in different memory places and times. She enjoys the long view. Her spirit is released into living through her dance. She is a dancer.

As she gets older she inhabits her body more and more comfortably; she has become at home in her body. She sees the capacities of the body being limited by the roles ascribed to it and the narratives by which we construct our lives (Andrews). She knows that these role boundaries do not map her experience or desires, her past and futures. She practices. She knows how practice can effect change in her body, in her movement, in her mind. She knows that working in her mind can effect change in her practice. She sees that her practice is integral to her living a life

of movement, growth and change. She observes how her practice has shifted from being instrumental as a young person to becoming intrinsic to her middle and old age. She imagines … seeing the invisible. She is become an artist.

In dancing and singing she observes how others are transformed. She observes how dancing and singing are transformative in herself. She knows that the dance can dance you (Tully). She wants to know more.

To conclude

Along with Dickie and many dancers of diverse backgrounds and ages, I continue to study ballet class with veteran ballet teacher Roger Tully who is now aged 85. It is a life class; these words are from his reflections on classical dancing, *The Song Sings the Bird*:

> " The physical forms of the dance are expressions of movements that have taken place elsewhere, either mentally or spiritually. To work only on the physical plane may effectively block out these finer movements" (Tully 16).

Acknowledgements

I am grateful to the participants in the research for their generous contributions and reflections, and to Roger Tully and Patrick Wood for their inspirational classes and thoughts.

The 2012 performance as research was supported using public funding by the National Lottery through Arts Council England, University of Surrey School of Arts, and Pump-priming funds.

References

Anderson, Lea. Personal interview. 4 January 2011.

Andrews, Molly. "The narrative complexity of successful aging". *Time to Move Conference; Take Art;* Tacchi-Morris Arts Centre, Taunton. *International Journal of Sociology and Social Policy.* 2009. Print.

Bethune, Lucy. Message to Jennifer Jackson. 9 January 2011. Email.

Bohm, David. *Wholeness and the Implicate Order.* London & New York: Routledge, 2005. Print.

Csikszentmihalyi, Mihaly. *Creativity: Flow and the psychology of discovery and invention.* New York: Harper Collins, 1996. Print.

Claxton, Guy. *Hare Brain Tortoise Mind: why intelligence increases when you think less.* London: Fourth Estate, 1998. Print.

Dickie, Ann. Personal Interview. 29 December 2010.

Ehrenreich, Barbara. *Dancing in the Streets: A history of collective joy.* London: Granta Books, 2007. Print.

Forsythe, William. *I think the body likes to move.* Dir. Anne Quirynen, Vlaams Theater Institut, Holland.1990. Film.

Hay Deborah. *Lamb at the Altar: The Story of a Dance.* Durham and London: Duke University Press, 1994.

Jackson. Jennifer. "My dance and my ideal body". *Research in Dance Education* 6, Issue1.2, April/December. (2005): 25–40.

Kay, Jackie. Interview. *Front Row.* BBC Radio 4. 4 January 2011. Radio.

John-Steiner, Vera. *Creative Collaboration.* NY: Oxford University Press, 2000. Print.

Lansley, Jacky and Fergus Early. *The Wise Body: conversations with experienced dancers.* Bristol UK: Intellect Books, 2011. Print.

Nakamura, Jeanne and Csikszentmihalyi, Mihaly. "Creativity In Later Life". *Creativity and Development.* Keith Sawyer. Ed. Oxford University Press. 2003. Ebook.

Potter, Lauren. Message to Jennifer Jackson. 8 January 2011. Email.

Rice. Simon. Personal Interview. 4 January 2011.

Sawyer, Keith. *Group Genius; the creative power of collaboration.* NY: Basic Books, 2007.

Tully, Roger. *The Song Sings the Bird: a manual on classical dancing.* Rome: Gremese, 2011. Print.

JENNIFER JACKSON

Jennifer is Senior Lecturer at the University of Surrey and teaches choreography at the Royal Ballet School. A former dancer and choreographer with the Royal Ballet and Sadlers Wells Royal Ballet, she has taught workshops and presented her research into the somatic exploration of ballet at conferences in USA, Australia, Sweden and Japan. Her current performance practice as a mature dancer develops from research into improvisation and somatic approaches to creating with ballet. Her choreography for mature performers, Dancing the Invisible, was given at the Ivy Arts Centre, Guildford in 2012. Other practice as research choreography includes Retrieving the Sylph (2013), a 'women choreographing on pointe' initiative for Counterpointe, Time Chant (2011) and Other Diamonds (2010) for English National Ballet. Recent performances include Late Work (2012/13) and The improbabilities of new ballet (2014). Her writing is published in professional and academic journals including Dancing Times and Research in Dance Education.

©2014 Royal Academy of Dance Enterprises Ltd
First published in 2014

Published by Royal Academy of Dance Enterprises Ltd
for Royal Academy of Dance 2014
36, Battersea Square
London SW11 3RA
t: +44 (0)20 7326 8080
e: sales@rad.org.uk
www.radenterprises.co.uk
www.rad.org.uk

Royal Academy of Dance Enterprises Ltd is a company
incorporated in England No.2773495. It gifts its annual
profits to the Royal Academy of Dance, a charity
registered in England and Wales No.312826.

VAT Reg No.GB603176371

ISBN 978-1-906980-23-8

Designed by Smith & Gilmour

Printed by Halstan